A WARTIME JOURNEY REVISITED

A WARTIME JOURNEY REVISITED

including
An Odyssey through Occupied Europe in 1943
by Pieter Schagen

IAN AND SANDIE SCHAGEN

Matador
9 Priory Business Park,
Wistow Road, Kibworth Beauchamp,
Leicestershire. LE8 0RX
Tel: 0116 279 2299
Email: books@troubador.co.uk
Web: www.troubador.co.uk/matador
Twitter: @matadorbooks

ISBN 978 1788037 709

British Library Cataloguing in Publication Data.
A catalogue record for this book is available from the British Library.

Printed and bound by CPI Group (UK) Ltd, Croydon, CR0 4YY
Typeset in 11pt Minion Pro by Troubador Publishing Ltd, Leicester, UK

Matador is an imprint of Troubador Publishing Ltd

In memory of Pieter Schagen, and his companions on the journey
With grateful thanks to all who helped them achieve their goal

Contents

Acknowledgements

We wish to record our grateful thanks to all those who enabled us to achieve our dream of telling this story. Our friend Renée Wachtel-Bech, widow of Theo Wachtel, provided invaluable help with our research and translated many of the Dutch documents. Joe Shillito and his colleagues at Troubador Publishing brought the book to publication, and are responsible for its professional appearance.

We would especially like to record our gratitude to those who helped with either of the two journeys described in this book. On our travels we were privileged to meet descendants of some of the people who gave Piet and Frans vital assistance or shelter on their way. In particular we would like to mention:

- Frans van der Sande, son of Suuske van der Sande who sheltered Piet and Frans, of Ossendrecht, Netherlands
- Eugene Jansen, grandson of Hugo Jansen who sheltered Piet and Frans, of Hoogerheide, Netherlands
- François Vanneufville, grandson of the farmer who sheltered Piet and Frans, and his wife Joséphine, of Lihu Farm, Lihons, France
- Mme Odinot, daughter of Mme Passaret who sheltered Piet and Frans, and her husband, of Toulouse, France
- Bernard and Marcel Standaert, grandsons of Séraphin Standaert who sheltered Piet and Frans, of Astaffort, France.

The other people who helped us are too numerous to mention, and we do not have all of their names! But they include:

- Richard Dekker, proprietor of Hotel Dekker in Ossendrecht, Netherlands, and the lady staying there when we visited
- Annie and her colleague at the Mairie in S Georges sur la Prée, France, and the couple living opposite who gave us hospitality and information
- Armelle, manager of 'Le Rail' café in Quiévrain, Belgium.

There were many other people – some unnamed, and some whose relatives we could not trace – who helped Piet and Frans on their journey. We express our thanks to them, and hope that the spirit of helping the stranger and the refugee will never die out.

Introduction

On 22 June 1943, two young men set off from Zaandam, a small Dutch town just north of Amsterdam. Pieter (Piet) Schagen, aged 27, had been a soldier in the Dutch army, which was overrun by the Nazis in 1940[1]. Dutch soldiers had been sent home, but in 1943 there was a plan to round them up and send them to forced labour camps. Piet heard of this and decided to escape. His companion was Frans van den Brink, aged 20, whom Piet had only recently met. Piet's aim was to join the Allied forces in England, although his plan was not clearly formulated at the start. Getting to England was to involve a long overland journey through Belgium and France, across the Pyrenees to Spain and finally via Portugal to Gibraltar.

On 16 August 2015, two people set off on the same journey: Piet's son Ian Schagen and his wife Sandie. Piet had written a book about his adventures, which he called *An odyssey through occupied Europe in 1943*. Ian had long cherished the wish to trace his father's journey, and now at last he had the opportunity to do so. His aim was to find the places mentioned in the book, and ideally meet descendants of some of the people named.

* * *

Although we wanted to follow as closely as possible in Piet's footsteps, there were of course many differences between our journey and his. The world had changed over the past 72 years, and we were much older (and less fit!) than Piet was when he was travelling. Our journey was much

---

1   See Appendix A for more details of his early life.

shorter: Piet took seven months to reach Gibraltar, we did it in two. Piet had to travel in secret, afraid of being caught by German soldiers or the local police. We had no such problem.

Piet and Frans had rucksacks, but that was all. We tried to travel light, but in practice that meant one case instead of two. We also carried cameras, a camcorder and a laptop, so we were able to record our journey in a way that Piet could not.

Piet used three modes of travel: train, hitching lifts and walking. Whenever possible, we did the same. We are now well acquainted with the Dutch, Belgian, French and Spanish railways! But we could not always travel in the way that Piet did. We enjoy walking – but not with all our luggage. So while we did cover many miles on foot, walking from A to B (as Piet sometimes did) was not feasible. We had to have a base where we could leave our luggage, and then get on the road. We were not prepared to hitchhike, so for the first part of the journey (where Piet relied mainly on lifts) we hired a car. This became necessary in a few other places, where lack of public transport made car hire the only way to reach certain destinations.

Friendly farmers often gave Piet a place to spread his sleeping bag for the night. We had the comparative luxury of small hotels. Piet's only money came from the sale of his stamp collection in Holland – and he lost half of that when changing Dutch guilders into Belgian francs. He often had to rely on the generosity of others. We had more money to start with, and no need to change currency – it was euros all the way until we reached Gibraltar.

The biggest difference, of course, was that Europe was at war in 1943, but thankfully not in 2015. It is hard now to imagine the dangers and difficulties involved in travelling through Europe during the war, although living Piet's book certainly helped us to do so. For him, crossing borders was a major problem – not only borders between countries, but between occupied and Vichy France. Now, thanks to the Schengen agreement, we travelled through five European countries with no evident borders, except for perhaps a 'Welcome to…' sign. The only time we had to produce our passports was when hotel receptionists asked to see them, but that did not happen often.

One thing we did have in common with Piet was that we received assistance from many people. He was grateful to those who gave him food, accommodation or transport, and those who helped him avoid the authorities. We did not need that kind of support, but there were many people who aided us in other ways: by giving directions, helping us find places or search out information, storing our luggage, offering their time and hospitality. We feel we made many friends on our travels.

In trying to locate people or places, we had another great advantage – the Internet. We used this to do some research before starting on our journey. In particular, we tried to trace companions mentioned in Piet's book: just Frans as far as Toulouse, but several others that he met while crossing the Pyrenees and later in Spanish prisons. We realised that 72 years on, most if not all would be dead, but there was just a chance that Frans in particular (since he was younger than Piet) might still be alive.

There is a Dutch association called 'Engelandvaarders[2]', for those who escaped (by whatever route) to England during World War II. We contacted them, and several other organisations, in the hope of tracing the men themselves, or their relatives. We pursued suggested avenues which sadly led us nowhere, but we did have one great stroke of luck. We made contact with Renée Wachtel-Bech, the second wife (now widow) of Theo Wachtel, one of the men Piet met in Spain. We exchanged information and photos, and Renée helped us enormously, not only by searching Dutch sources on our behalf, but also by translating papers for us.

At the start of his book, Piet wrote a foreword:

This is the story of a wartime trek through occupied Europe to the Allied camp in Britain, undertaken by two young men from the town of Zaandam in North Holland, a few miles north of Amsterdam, in order to serve their Queen and country in the Netherlands Royal Navy and Air Force.

As these reminiscences are of a personal nature this story is written in the first person and has no pretence of any literary worth, nor of grammatical correctness, spelling or punctuation.

It has been compiled, years after the events, from memories of the participants, strengthened by notes taken shortly after reaching the safety of neutral territory.

---

2   The word actually means 'England paddlers', as many of the earlier escapers paddled across the North Sea.

The experiences here described cannot be compared with those of like-minded compatriots not having had the same good fortune.

Nor must be forgotten the efforts made by those who tried, but did not succeed, in reaching their goal. Many lost their life in the attempt or fell into the hands of the ever vigilant enemy to suffer internment or extinction. Some however survived their privations.

May they, known and unknown, not be forgotten.

It was a great adventure, one that we will never forget. We learned a lot, and succeeded beyond our expectations. This is the story of our journey, and Piet's.

Note about Piet's account

Piet wrote the story of his travels for the family, using an early word processor with no spell checker. English was not his first language, although he became extremely proficient in it. We have done a minimal amount of editing while transferring his story to this book, correcting spelling and improving grammar only where necessary to make the meaning of sentences clearer. Otherwise we have tried to let Piet's individual voice come through in his own account.

Pieter Schagen
(Spain 1943)

Chapter 1

The Netherlands – the journey begins

On 13 August 2015 we flew from London to Amsterdam, in preparation for our journey south to Gibraltar, following the route taken by Ian's father Piet in 1943. Before setting off, we spent three days in Zaandam, a small town close to Amsterdam on the other side of the North Sea Canal. Our main aim was to trace Frans van den Brink, who was Piet's travelling companion.

Frans van den Brink and I met for the very first time in the small township of Valkenswaard in the Province of North Brabant, only a small distance from the Dutch-Belgian border. It was a day in the middle of June 1943 and our country was under the heel of the German occupying forces and administration.

The farmer who allowed me to spread my sleeping bag in his hayloft told me that there were already three backpackers there but that they had gone out to do some shopping.

Just then, when I had installed myself, the threesome arrived. One was a young man of about 20 years of age and the others were two girls. I recognised one of the girls as the ex-fiancée of a friend. The other was the young man's sister. They were all from my home town Zaandam.

After some careful inquiring, from both sides, as to the reason of us being so far from home, it transpired that they were looking for a safe place for Frans, who expected a call to be sent to work in Germany at any moment.

I had been a Dutch prisoner of war[1] about to be rounded up to be returned to a POW camp in Germany; a prospect I did not cherish overmuch.

Frans van den Brink

Piet already had the idea of getting to England, and joining the Allied forces, but he did not at first confess this to the others. He told them that he was making for the woods in Northern France where he had heard that there was work and a better hiding place than in the Netherlands. It was agreed that Frans would go with him, *'as he had done naughty deeds against the occupying forces and may be looked for'.*

But first they would return to Zaandam to *'get Frans better kitted out for a prolonged stay in France and meet again at eight on the morning of the 22nd of June outside Zaandam railway station'.*

Being younger than Piet, Frans would have been 92 by 2015, and possibly still alive. Attempts to trace him via the Internet had given us three possible addresses, two in Zaandam. We went to the city hall, but they were unable to find him in their records. We looked in the phone book, found half a dozen van den Brinks, and tried calling them all, but those who answered said they knew nothing of Frans.

The other address we had been given was in Heerhugowaard, a town to the north of Zaandam. Our friend Renée Wachtel-Bech had already established that the current occupants had a different name, but we thought they might have bought the house from Frans and might know where he was now. Even if he was dead, they might possibly know where his relatives lived. We thought it would be easier to have this conversation if we went and knocked on their door. Unfortunately, we did not get that

---

1   On arriving in London Piet reported his army experience to the Dutch authorities (see Appendix A). He does not mention being a prisoner of war, but perhaps he was considered to be one after the Dutch army capitulated in 1940.

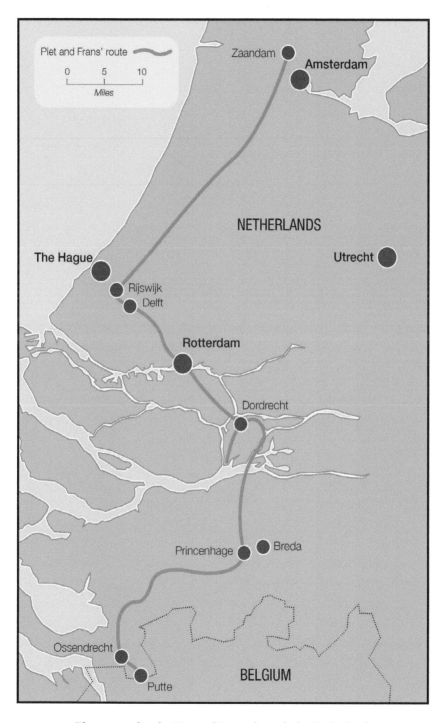

The route taken by Piet and Frans through the Netherlands

Research in the NIOD

far! The address was not a house, but a flat in a block with entry-phones. We rang the number, and tried asking about Frans van den Brink, but all we got was a curt *'He's dead'* and then were cut off.

So our last hope of tracing Frans – or his relatives – was gone. However, although we could not find Frans himself, we did find his writing! Renée had discovered that the Netherlands Institute for War, Genocide and Holocaust Studies (NIOD) in Amsterdam had a 'little diary' written by Frans. We went there, and found that it was staffed by friendly and helpful people who spoke extremely good English. This was just as well, as Sandie's Dutch is non-existent and Ian's has virtually disappeared in the sixty years since he left Holland. After we had signed in and acquired official reader's cards (the first of several we collected on our travels), we were shown the original hand-written diary in which Frans recorded his journey with Piet. It was very short, and written in Dutch, but it gave us a thrill to turn the pages and know this was an actual relic of that time and an independent account of their odyssey. We also saw a folder with some materials relating to Piet, including a

Ian, Fita and Pieter

summary of an interview he had with the Dutch authorities once he reached London[2].

The NIOD sent us electronic copies of these documents, and later Renée translated them for us. We refer to Frans's diary occasionally, where it supplements the information in Piet's account.

While in Zaandam, we visited Ian's Aunt Fita, Piet's youngest sister (who died while this book was in preparation). We were accompanied by Ian's cousin Pieter and his wife Heather; they live in Australia but were on a tour of Europe. This was fortunate, as Pieter still speaks Dutch and was able to interpret. Among other things, Fita told us that after Piet had left home on his odyssey, the Germans came for him. The family feigned total ignorance, and said they had no idea where he was – he might even be dead, for all they knew. He obviously made his escape just in time!

---

2   We now know that there was more than one interview – see Appendix A. The document we saw at NIOD reported the first one, about the economic circumstances in occupied countries.

Setting off on the journey

Our final mission in Zaandam was to find the route taken by Piet and Frans when they left the town. Piet writes:

> *We did meet at the agreed place and time and set out on foot southward towards the ferry across the large canal which connects Amsterdam to the North Sea.*
>
> *We had agreed that as backpackers we would at all times be of the neatest appearance we could manage and that our pack would be neat and tidy with our rucksacks squared and no loose equipment hanging from the outside. At no time should we be mistaken for vagabonds as we could not expect a good reception as scruffy individuals.*

We wanted to set off as they did, and walk as far as the ferry. But where was it? At the Zaandam tourist office we asked about the ferry across the North Sea Canal, to be assured that the only ferry was a small passenger boat which ran from a jetty in Zaandam to Amsterdam. Other people said the same. We knew that the ferry they referred to could not be the one in Piet's book, since it was in the wrong direction from the railway station, and did not carry cars, as his did. We reasoned that Piet's ferry had possibly been replaced by a bridge in the years since 1943, but nobody was able to confirm this. After studying maps – and talking to a woman in the railway station café – we set off to walk south in the direction of Hembrug, on the canal. We followed a major road with signs to Hembrug and other places. Suddenly we gasped with excitement. The sign just ahead of us included a ferry symbol! Soon afterwards we reached the banks of the wide North Sea Canal, where there was a ferry landing, with cars, bikes and foot passengers waiting to cross. Then the ferry itself appeared, chugging towards us from the south bank.

We boarded with the other foot passengers and crossed the river. On the way we studied the plaque with details of the vessel, and found that it was built in 1952, so not the actual boat that

Old Zaandam station

Piet and Frans used. But it was certainly the right ferry. This was the first, but not the last, time that we proved the accuracy of Piet's book, finding evidence of something that people had told us did not exist.

From the ferry, Piet and Frans were able to get a series of lifts:

> *At the ferry our luck was in as we obtained a lift from Mr Bruynzeel, a Zaandam businessman who took us in his car all the way to Rijswijk on the outskirts of The Hague. There was an air-raid alarm and all the traffic had to stop until the all clear. We managed to continue our journey on the back of a lorry loaded with milk churns to the next town of Delft, where again we had the luck to be taken by another milk lorry to Rotterdam. There we waited a while before a truck and trailer, loaded with roof tiles, took us aboard with destination south of the large rivers to Brabant.*

After our very short ferry crossing, we landed and saw the road heading southward, clearly the route taken by Mr Bruynzeel and his passengers.

South to Brabant

On Sunday 16 August we left Zaandam and took the train back to the airport, where we hired a car, in order to pursue Piet and Frans southward.

The ferry that didn't exist

We drove past The Hague, Delft and Rotterdam, as far as the town of Dordrecht.

Piet reports:

At the Moerdijk road bridge we were stopped by a German sentry as no passengers were to cross the bridge. We had to return to Dordrecht from where we took a bus to the ferry across the Moerdijk to Lage Zwaluwe from where we managed our last lift of the day on a lorry taking vegetables to the market at Princenhage near Breda. We found shelter for the night at a farm and considered ourselves very lucky to have come this far without spending a large amount on fares.

As Piet did, we drove south across the Moerdijk road bridge to the province of Brabant. Next to the bridge is the village of Moerdijk, where we parked briefly to get a view of the stretch of water which Piet calls the Moerdijk. The current map calls it the 'Hollands Diep', and it is one of the channels of the estuary of the Rhine. We had failed to find any information about the ferry Piet mentions, so we drove to Lage Zwaluwe (east of the bridge) to see if we could get any clues there.

We could find no tourist information, but went into the village bar and asked if anyone knew about a ferry that used to terminate there. A man told us that there used to be a ferry during the war, for Dutch people only, that ran from Kop van 't Land, east of Dordrecht, to Lage Zwaluwe. So once again we found confirmation of Piet's account. We were to discover during our journey that the local bar was often the best place to get information!

From Lage Zwaluwe there is a narrow road that runs along the bank of the river and under the bridge back to Moerdijk, and we drove along it to get a better view of the bridge. We found an old bunker near the bridge, another relic of the war.

Breda is a large town a few miles south of Lage Zwaluwe, and Princenhage is on its western outskirts. We had no way of finding the farm where Piet and Frans stayed, though Piet's later mention of Roosendaal confirms that it was to the west of Breda.

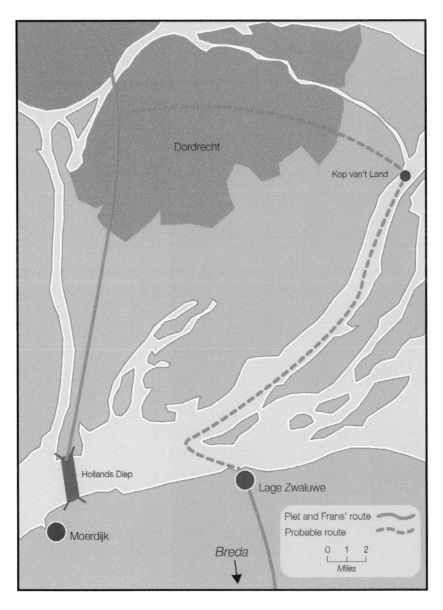

Dordrecht to Breda

Ossendrecht

The next morning, after having made our toilet, we thanked our host, walked to the main road to Roosendaal where we were in luck again to be picked up by an official of the Labour Exchange in Bergen op Zoom who set us off at its outskirts. It was now raining cats and dogs while we were waiting at the roadside for our next lift. A lorry, loaded with sacks of potatoes, took us as far as the cross roads near Ossendrecht. The torrential rain had stopped and we marched to the café Bolders which I knew well from my service as an auxiliary customs officer in the years 1940-41[3]. I also knew the border well. That night we stayed at the homestead of Suuske van Zanden, a known smuggler, who warned us against crossing at Ossendrecht and advised us to go and see forester Huybrechts in the woods of Putte.

On 17 August we drove down to Ossendrecht, a small town not far from the Belgian border. We began looking for a tourist office or library, but without much success. Then someone suggested we go to the Hotel Dekker, in the centre of town, and ask there. The owner, Richard Dekker, was amazingly helpful. He gave us a map of the town and told us that the Café Bolders, which Piet mentions, actually stood opposite but had been demolished and replaced by another building – he pointed out the site to us through the window.

Furthermore, he told us that there was an old lady staying in the hotel who had lived there for a long time and who might be able to help us. He knocked on her door, but she was out, and he suggested we came back later. We went for a stroll round the town, and found the library – which was closed. On our return to Hotel Dekker we sat in the bar and had coffee and apple cake with whipped cream – a Dutch speciality.

Richard Dekker took us to see the lady and her husband, who were now in, and interpreted for us while we told our story and asked questions. The lady made a phone call and told us that Frans van der Sande, son of the Suuske who helped Piet, was on his way over to meet us! Frans duly arrived on his bicycle, and we spent some time in the bar while he told us about the town and his father. He said that Suuske was

---

3   According to the information he gave when interviewed by the Dutch authorities in London (see Appendix A), Piet became a customs officer in 1940, but was based to Ossendrecht 1941-2.

Meeting Frans van der Sande

not a smuggler in our sense of the word, just a farmer who happened to trade across the border. Then he offered to show us some of the places in the neighbourhood which were mentioned in Piet's book.

The three of us went for a drive, with Frans pointing out places of interest. He showed us where the customs office used to be – where Piet would have worked in the early 1940s. Next we passed the farm of Hugo Jansen, now passed on to grandchildren, and after that reached his father's old farm, where Piet and Frans stayed for the first night. From there we drove down to the village of Putte, which straddles the border, and he showed us the border marker, number 247, on the street which forms the frontier between the Netherlands and Belgium. He said that a customs officer often stood there to check goods coming across, so it seemed likely that Piet may have been on duty at that very spot.

We returned to Ossendrecht and the bar of the Hotel Dekker, and Frans showed us a book about the Jansen family history, produced by the son of Hugo Jansen, and gave us his address in Hoogerheide, a nearby town. (We traced Eugene Jansen next day; unfortunately he spoke little English, but he gave us two photos of his parents' wedding.)

Finally we said goodbye to Frans, thanking him profusely, and he went off on his bike. We also thanked Richard Dekker, and went to find the hotel we had booked, in the woods near Ossendrecht. That turned out to be a centre for walking and cycling, and they showed us lots of maps of the woods in the local area. They telephoned a nearby centre for us, and we were able to go and get the maps we needed to navigate a route through the woods to Belgium next day.

We had not been able to find any trace of Forester Huybrechts. We looked in the phone book for Putte and found four people with that name, so we drove back there in the late afternoon. We knocked on doors at the addresses we had found, but only three answered and none admitted to knowing anything of Forester Huybrechts in 1943. Our lack of Dutch was doubtless a handicap for this task. We had dinner at a restaurant called 'Taverne Grenszicht' situated next to the border marker, and marvelled at the contrast between the strict border controls in 1943 and the situation in 2015. Now the Belgian flag is flying just across the street, and people are driving or walking freely to and fro between the two countries. The waitress told us that many of the people who live in the Dutch half of Putte send their children to school in Belgium *'because the schools are better'*.

The woods of Putte

The next day we left our goods and chattels at Suuske and went to see the forester but on the way were stopped by two policemen who warned us that we were within two miles of the frontier and forbidden territory for those without a proper German pass. We therefore returned to Ossendrecht and stayed overnight at the farm of Hugo Jansen. His sister, the widow van der Venne, was too nervous to give us shelter. At Hugo we peeled a mountain of peas to pay for his hospitality.

It was now Friday morning and we went again to see the forester but to avoid the roads we went through the woods. The forester was most helpful and pointed out a stretch of woodland that went straight into Belgium. We then made up our minds to try the crossing at noon that day as I expected that the border guards would be changing shifts. But as it was we were intercepted when we were already on Belgian territory by a Dutch policeman, a Mr Feenstra, who "because we were obviously lost" sent us back to Holland. (Later, after the war was over, he wrote to Frans asking how we got on after he left us. I wrote to him but my letter was returned "unknown at the address".)

We waited for about a half hour, hidden in the undergrowth, until we deemed the coast to be clear. We managed to get a good way into Belgium and were shown the direction to Berendrecht by two women rummaging in the woods.

The following day we set out to walk through the woods near Putte to cross the border to Berendrecht in Belgium. We could not determine exactly the route that Piet and Frans took, but it seemed likely that it was due east through the woods just north of Putte. We parked in the town and walked up the road, until we reached a Jewish cemetery. We went to have a look inside, and found a monument to the victims of the Holocaust. This was quite moving, especially as we remembered that many of the others fleeing from Nazi-occupied Europe alongside Piet were Jews trying to escape the death camps.

Opposite the cemetery was a straight path through the woods heading due east, so off we went. It brought us past a large open area, and then through more woods to a familiar-looking border marker. Once past that, we were in Belgium. We carried on, emerged from the woods, walked under a motorway, and reached Berendrecht. After a brief look round, and a fruitless search for a café, we left Berendrecht and headed back towards Putte along a different path.

On the way we reached an impressive chateau called Ravenhof. Luckily it had a café, because by then we were hungry! We walked into Putte along the border street, and then turned north, back to the Netherlands, the car and our hotel.

Through the woods at Putte

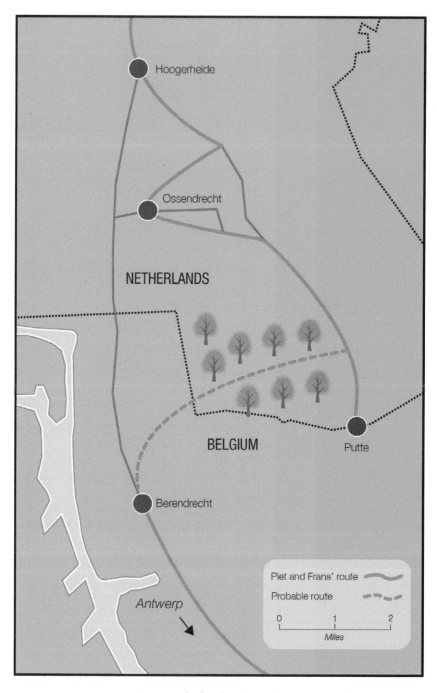

Crossing the border into Belgium

Chapter 2

Belgium

fter walking across the border through the woods, Piet and Frans reached the village of Berendrecht in Belgium.

There we knocked on the door of a little house and met a woman I remembered from my customs days. She too remembered me letting her and her daughter with a sack of potatoes through. Here at her home we refreshed ourselves, changed our Dutch guilders into Belgian francs (at a 50% loss) and waited for the tram to Antwerp to be due. The tram took us to Antwerp railway station where we boarded a fast train to Brussels.

In Berendrecht there are no longer trams to Antwerp, though we did find a bus stop with regular buses going there. The other change from 1943 is that you no longer have to change money every time you cross a border – long live the euro!

Antwerp and Brussels

On 19 August we left Ossendrecht and the Netherlands, and drove down through Putte into Belgium, and on towards Antwerp. All went well until we reached the city limits and found that one of the main bridges was closed and traffic was being diverted with no clear indication of which way to go. After some random driving we managed to find our way into the city, and parked with a sigh of relief.

Antwerp Central Station

Piet and Frans did not spend long in Antwerp – they arrived at the station and caught the first train to Brussels. We visited the central railway station, which is an impressive baroque edifice. Inside we discovered the more modern part of the station has platforms on three levels – presumably to save space.

Since it was our first time in the city, we decided to have a 'day off' from our research and do some sightseeing. The following day we drove to Brussels. We had decided to take the car rather than the train so that we could more easily explore the outskirts of Brussels for the garages that Piet mentions.

In Brussels I knew a Monsieur Lauwers to whom I had rendered a "service" in the past. He was the owner of two garages: one in the Rue Stephenson and the other in the Rue d'Anethan. We located him eventually in the latter. There we left our packs and took only our overnight kit to his home in the Rue de l'Imperatrice in Meijsse, where I met his wife and daughter again. After supper we talked to late into the night and slept between sheets.

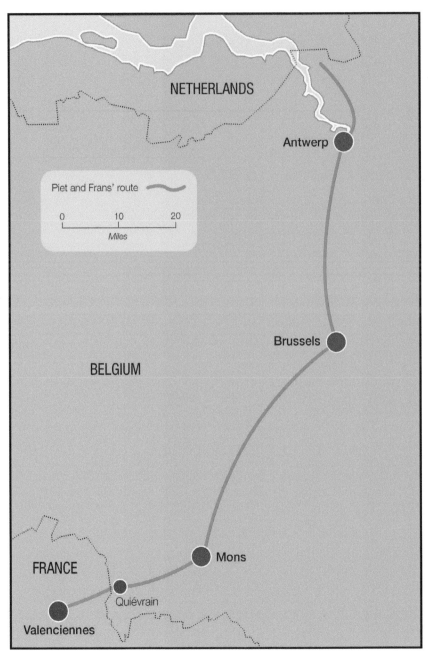

The route taken by Piet and Frans through Belgium

The next morning we collected our stuff from the Rue D'Anethan and deposited it at the left luggage office at Gare du Midi to be picked up later. With M. Lauwers' daughter as guide we did some sightseeing in Brussels, not forgetting the little man at the corner of a square, before we had to be at the station as our train south would be leaving at one o'clock. The train left on time for its destination Mons and further on to Quiévrain, the last stop before the Belgian-French border. The tickets were a parting gesture of M. Lauwers.

It would be fascinating to discover what the 'service' was that Piet rendered to M Lauwers, but there is no hint in the book. Presumably it was connected with his time in the customs service on the border.

We had found the two streets on the internet – they are close together in the north-eastern suburbs of the city. We parked nearby and began to explore on foot. We soon found a garage in the Rue d'Anethan, but the people inside said it was certainly not there in 1943. It was a similar story in the Rue Stephenson – there was a garage, but clearly not the right one. Dispirited, we headed back to the car. Then we noticed a large building, clearly a garage, with the name 'Rauwers' emblazoned on it. It was in the wrong street, and the name was not quite right, but perhaps Piet had mis-remembered it? And maybe the family had expanded their business and moved to a new location between the two old garages?

Nervously we went inside and approached the information desk. Now we were in southern Belgium the language was French, so we tried in our best fractured French to explain our mission. The man said he would go and fetch the owner, who turned out to be delightfully helpful and spoke very good English. We explained our hypothesis, which he immediately squashed. He said that there definitely was a family Lauwers, as well as his own family of Rauwers, who ran garages in the past. To prove it he whipped out his smartphone and summoned up in a few keystrokes an image of an old invoice from 1944 with the name 'Lauwers & Marroyen', and an address of 122 Rue Stephenson! He said they had disappeared over the years and no longer existed in Brussels.

We thanked him profusely and hurried back to Rue Stephenson. At number 122 there was fairly new-looking building, so obviously the old

The Brussels Experience

garage had been demolished and replaced. But at least we now knew where it had been.

We drove on into Brussels and, after getting lost again, found the Gare du Midi and returned the hire car there. We took the metro to the city centre and checked into a fairly smart hotel. Although we had visited Brussels before, we felt that we should do the tourist thing as Piet did. We went up to the Gare du Nord to see where he arrived in the city, and visited the Mannekin Pis which he (rather coyly) mentions being taken to see. We went to the Grand Place (surrounded by impressive buildings topped with gold statues) and had drinks and Belgian waffles while watching the tourist hordes surge to and fro.

The following morning we went to the Archives of Belgium, which was close to our hotel. We were welcomed at reception and soon afterwards met by a pleasant young man called Filip, with whom we had corresponded by email. We explained our search for M Lauwers, but he was unable to find any more information about him. We talked about the difficulty of finding the address of his home – Rue de l'Imperatrice in Meijsse – as it was impossible to find on the Internet. He told us that the suburb was actually spelled Meise, and that the problem with the street might be due to a change of language. Back in the 1940s streets were all given French names (to avoid the German-sounding Flemish), but many had since been renamed. The Flemish equivalent of Rue de l'Imperatrice was Keizerinstraat. Later on we surfed for Keizerinstraat in Meise, and there it was! Another mystery solved.

Quiévrain and the border

We said grateful thanks to Filip, collected our luggage from the hotel, and

Arriving at Quiévrain

dragged the case back over the cobbled streets to the metro. We returned to the Gare du Midi and bought tickets to Quiévrain, down on the French border. After just over an hour we reached Quiévrain, the end of the line. The place looked very different in 1943.

Arriving at Quiévrain station we stood outside for a little while to get our bearings. In the square in front of the station building stood an old-fashioned steam tram waiting for the last passengers to emerge from the station. Then it left with a whistle and soon disappeared in the streets of the town.

Opposite the station was a row of cafés, some with names in French but one bore the name "'t Witte konijn" (The White Rabbit) in Flemish. That was the one we made for as we assumed Flemish might be spoken there. We entered the pub and I ordered two small beers much to the distress of Frans who had been brought up in a teetotal family. But there was nothing for it: When in Belgium do as the Belgians – drink beer!

When she wasn't busy I approached the lady behind the bar to ask if I could have a word in confidence and was invited to the room behind the bar where I confided to her that we wanted to cross the border into France bypassing the German frontier post. Could she help? With a broad grin she told me of our 'great fortune' as in the taproom was 'the greatest smuggler of the district' and she would have a word with him. As good as her word she went over to a man sitting in conversation with two elderly ladies. Shortly he came over to us and introduced himself as 'Martin from Rotterdam' but now living in France. The two ladies with him were aunts from Holland who had come over for his daughter's wedding. After ordering more beer (poor Frans!) he informed us that he would first take the two aunts on the next train to his farm across the border and then come back to bring us across. Not from here but a short tram ride away.

In 2015, the station building was derelict, and clearly the tram line was long gone. There was a bus stop next to the station and a wide empty square with some buildings opposite. Of the 'row of cafés' that Piet describes, a single café only remained, with the name 'Le Rail' over the window. Under that we could see other faint letters, but peer as we might we were unable to decipher what previous names it might have had. Slightly disappointed, we went inside and ordered drinks. Like her predecessor, the 'lady behind the bar' was very helpful, although neither she nor the others present could tell us anything about the 'White Rabbit' café.

Piet continues:

We had to take the 9 o'clock tram from the square to Roisin. We should pay the conductor, who would be in the know, for two singles to Roisin. He would put us off the tram and direct us further to Luis Ruez's café in the woods. He would pick us up from there.

The nine o'clock tram arrived, we boarded, paid the smiling and winking conductor and settled down. At every halt we looked at the conductor who shook his head so we stayed in our seats until we came to the halt outside a whitewashed pub where he nodded. We alighted and so did the tram man who took us inside the café. After ordering a round of beers he began to explain how to reach our rendez-vous with Martin. My school-French was no match for his Walloon French, so after we had finished our beer he borrowed a bicycle from the pub and escorted us up the hill, whilst the tram stayed waiting patiently. We reached a crossing of five paths and were shown the right one. He now mounted the bike and coasted down the hill to where the tram stood waiting, parked the bike against the pub and got aboard and the tram moved off with a cheerful whistle. What the passengers thought of this will remain a question.

Our barmaid's name was Armelle, and she became a good friend to us. She said there was now a bus to Roisin, so we decided to head there and try to find the place where Piet and Frans left the tram. However, when we checked the bus timetable it seemed that there was no bus for quite a while, so we thought we would start walking the five miles or so. Armelle gladly agreed to look after our luggage for us, and off we went.

From Quiévrain, the road went south towards Roisin, roughly parallel with the French border a mile or so to the west. We were looking out for a place matching Piet's description – where a path through the woods runs uphill away from the road to the west. However, the land westwards seemed flat, and not very wooded. We reached the little village of Basieux after a mile or so, and then a car stopped and a man offered us a lift, which we were happy to accept. On the way we tried to locate places where the tram might have dropped Piet and Frans, but without any success. On reaching Roisin we thanked our kind driver, and had a look round the village.

Soon it was time for the bus back to Quiévrain, so we returned to the station, somewhat frustrated by our failure to identify Piet's route. Back at Le Rail we had a drink, or two, and Sandie developed a fondness for one of the local beers. We asked about accommodation in Quiévrain, and discovered there was none at all – the nearest hotel was in the village of Thulin. Armelle phoned and reserved a room for us at the 'Auberge 19th Century' there. We said goodbye to her, and arranged to come back in the morning to do more research, on foot.

We caught the train back towards Brussels, and got off at Thulin, the next stop. The station was about half a mile from the village centre, where we found the hotel. Although not cheap, it was very pleasant with good food and what we recognised as a typical small-town French hotel atmosphere.

The next morning we took the train back to Quiévrain. We waited outside the café for Armelle to arrive, after walking her dog, and we left our luggage with her again. Then it was south on foot again, still searching for the place where the tram dropped off Piet and Frans. This

Uphill to the border

time we walked through Basieux and on to the next village of Angre. There we found a bar by the road, with the remains of some whitewash on the walls, which could have been the one Piet describes. We went in for a coffee, and tried to ask about the café of Louis Ruez, but were unable to get any information.

Just opposite the café was a side road, which sloped uphill towards the French border. We climbed up steadily until we reached a spot with a small shrine, where several paths and tracks converged together. This seemed to fit Piet's description of the place the tram driver led them to, except that there were hardly any trees. All around was open farmland, with some trees in the distance. We had no way of guessing which way the café in the woods might have lain, so we followed the road onwards, eventually passing through some trees and reaching the village of Marchipont, which straddles the border.

On the path to Ruez's café we met a Belgian customs officer pushing a bike laden with bulging sacks which from experience I recognised as a smuggler's haul. I bade him "Bon Soir" and continued our way until we reached the café in the woods. It was dark by now and we awaited Martin's arrival; but not without another beer. Shortly our guide arrived and we were treated to yet another beer; the fifth that evening! We had to change our walking boots to plimsolls so as to make less noise. We moved off in single file behind Martin in the pitch dark and eventually arrived at his farm.

There it was a hive of activity with the preparations for the forthcoming wedding. We also met again the two Dutch aunts, were treated to crepes and of all things brandy. Because of a shortage of beds Frans and I slept in deckchairs.

Marchipont village

On Sunday 27 June, the fifth day since our departure from home, we found ourselves in Northern France, having gone through two frontiers without much trouble, and were now in our third country, unscathed thanks to so many helpful people.

At Marchipont we crossed into France, but had no idea where the farm belonging to 'Martin from Rotterdam' might lie. We decided to return to Quiévrain by a track marked on the map, but that soon became overgrown and virtually impassable, so we turned back to Marchipont. From there we walked west, and reached a main road heading north to the village of Quiévrechain, on the French side of the border adjoining Quiévrain on the Belgian side.

As we crossed back into Belgium, we noticed that both sides of the road were lined with shops selling tobacco products, and had signs such as 'First Tobacco Shop in Belgium'. Clearly tobacco duty is much lower in Belgium than in France, and Quiévrain makes its living from French tobacco tourists. We stopped at a bar just across the border for much-

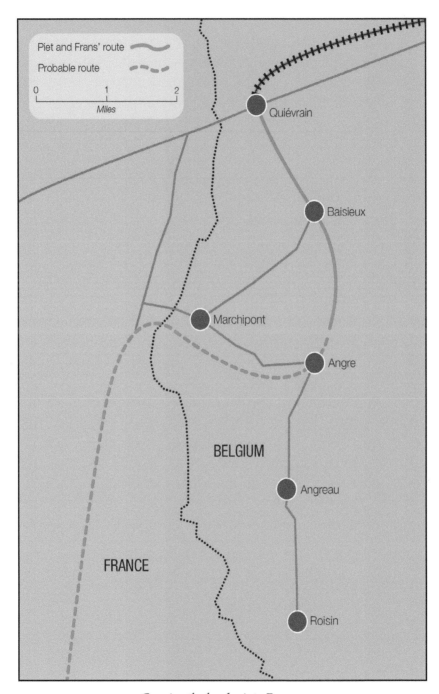

Crossing the border into France

needed liquid refreshment, and then walked back to the station and the Le Rail café to collect our luggage.

After saying a grateful goodbye to Armelle, we wheeled the case back through Quiévrain and across the border to the first bus stop on the French side. After a short wait, a bus took us into the town of Valenciennes and deposited us outside the station there. We had followed Piet and Frans into their third country, with far fewer difficulties than they experienced.

Chapter 3

Occupied France

Now in France, Piet and Frans continued their journey through occupied territory.

After breakfast and having been given two large parcels of food Martin brought us as far as the main road between Maubeuge and Valanciennes[4] where we parted. But not until he had given us a little note with: "de la part de M." on it and the address of the "Franco-Belge" pub in Valanciennes. Now came the most unforgettable experience of our trip so far, the "accolade". Anyone who has ever been kissed on freshly shaven cheeks by a French farmer with a seven day stubble will know what we suffered for our country.

We faced a march of some 10 miles and, it being a Sunday, there was no wheeled traffic at that time of day from which we could beg a ride. But by now we began to get used to the load we were carrying on our backs.

Frans, who had by now seen through my little invention of "work in the French woods" and that it was all eyewash, was quite happy with the idea of aiming for England if we could make it. The question arose: via Switzerland or Spain? Both were neutral countries, but where the first one was surrounded by enemy held territory it was foreseen that it could prove difficult to get away from there. On the other hand Spain was governed by the dictator General Franco and his party the "Falange". But it had on three sides the sea with its ports and also borders on neutral Portugal, from where it was possible to fly from Lisbon to Britain by a regular air service with KLM, our national airline. So Spain was the choice.

---

4   Piet spells the town 'Valanciennes', though the correct spelling is 'Valenciennes'.

Piet's analysis of the choices facing them seems accurate, and the decision made was the right one. This was proved later, when they crossed the Pyrenees, as some members of the party had actually come from Switzerland. His hopes of flying to Britain were to be dashed, however.

But in order to reach the Pyrenees, Piet and Frans had a long and dangerous journey through occupied France.

Valenciennes

We reached Valanciennes in the afternoon and, after some inquiries found the "Franco-Belge" pub. Martin's note was shown to the bartender and after conferring with one of the patrons we were conducted to the "Hotel des Voyageurs" opposite the railway station; the welcome was by Monsieur Ferdinand, the owner. He showed us upstairs to a room with a double bed and said that supper would be ready when we came down after having refreshed ourselves. After our exertions of the march we ate like wolves overseen by M. Ferdinand. That night we slept two to a bed and had no more worries.

Valenciennes station

We arrived in Valenciennes by bus from the Belgian border, and checked into Le Grand Hotel, opposite the railway station. We asked if this used to be the 'Hotel des Voyageurs', but were assured it had always had the same name. Another hotel nearby was too recent to be the one Piet and Frans stayed in. Near the station we found an estate agent's office with the title 'Hotel du Terminus' over the door. The building appeared to be the right age, and could have once been a hotel, but there was no way of checking that. We wondered if perhaps 'hotel des voyageurs' (travellers' hotel) was a description of the type of place, rather than a name, as Piet assumed. He continues:

> *Early the next morning we were called for breakfast as "our train would be leaving soon". During breakfast our host told us that he would be sending us on our way south, to a good friend, a World War One comrade, a Monsieur Vanneuville who lived on a farm called "Lihu" just outside the village of Lihons near the town of Chaulnes in Picardie. We had to memorise names and addresses as it would not be safe to commit these to paper. Before leaving I asked M. Ferdinand how much we owed him; his reply was: "Rien, come back after the war and pay me then". He then presented us with two single train tickets to Chaulnes.*
>
> *(After the war was over I did visit Valanciennes but there was no more "Monsieur Ferdinand")*

It is entirely possible that M Ferdinand was active in the Resistance and lost his life during the occupation.

> *After leaving Valanciennes via Amiens, where we had to change trains, we reached Chaulnes without either ticket control or a check on our papers. During our journey we went over our experiences again wondering how long our good luck would last as there were still some 500 miles, as the crow flies, to travel before we reached even the foothills of the Pyrenees.*
>
> *Between Valanciennes and Chaulnes we passed a great many WW1 war cemeteries, reminding us that we travelled through the battlefields of the Somme area.*
>
> *From Chaulnes we set off on foot to the hamlet of Lihons, and there asked our way to the Lihu farm. Wherever we went on foot the Michelin maps were of invaluable assistance; even the farm was on it.*

We caught the afternoon train from Valenciennes to Chaulnes, with a change at Amiens, and arrived at the little station in early evening, about 7pm. There was supposed to be a connecting bus to Hattencourt, where we had booked accommodation, but no bus appeared. We tried taxis, without success. Finally we telephoned the owner of the *chambre d'hote* and he kindly came and picked us up.

The farm Lihu

The following morning we caught the bus back to Chaulnes and set off on foot along the route to Lihons and the farm Lihu. Unfortunately it was pouring with rain, but we pressed on along the main road, with a break in a café in Lihons. As Piet says, the farm Lihu is marked on the Michelin map, and we found it easily, arriving just as the rain was slackening off. Piet gives a detailed description of the farm, where they received a warm welcome.

> *The farm, when we came to it, turned out to be a veritable stronghold. A very large walled square with turrets at the corners; medieval in looks. There was only one way in through a high double gate. Inside, and forming part of the outer wall was the stone-built two-storey main farmhouse. Also built into the outer wall were the dwellings of the farmworkers and their families together with storage and wagon sheds. It was a real stronghold reminding us of earlier times when Europe was overrun by marauding bands of disbanded mercenaries out looting and ravaging. Later we encountered other such lonely fortified farms.*
>
> *We called at the kitchen door of the main building to ask for our water bottles to be filled. When these were returned we found that they now contained wine. Taken aback I explained that we had very little money to pay for wine. But that was all right we were told; water was not good for drinking and the wine was free. So we would give the kitchen staff a song in appreciation. With Frans on guitar and harmonica and me on the mandolin we "treated" them to some of our old campfire songs. This drew the farmworkers' wives and their children out of their houses and also the lady of the house came to see what the commotion was about. This gave me the opportunity to ask after M. Vanneuville and bring him greetings from his erstwhile wartime comrade. We were asked into the house to*

await his return. Upon his homecoming a little later we were asked to stay and make some more "music". I explained that we had to find a place to stay for the night and also make our evening meal. This was set aside; we could have supper with them and stay for the night.

We had some more entertainment that evening after the meal. Some relatives or friends also turned up and from one we learned the lyrics of some well-known French songs of which we knew the tunes. The lyrics were written down for us to learn by heart. Our French was a source of amusement to the family. We were also made familiar with some usual [expressions]. M. Vanneuville could help us with a reliable address within a day's journey but suggested that the Dutch Consul in Roye might be of assistance to us.

When we reached the Lihu farm it was as impressive as Piet describes, set four-square in the open French countryside. The main farmhouse seemed in good repair; however, the outbuildings surrounding the central courtyard had gaping holes in the roof, and seemed in need of some upkeep. We took some photos and then knocked cautiously at the door of the main house.

When we explained, in our halting French, who we were and what we

Ferme de Lihu

wanted, we were welcomed inside. Our host turned out to be François, grandson of the farmer who sheltered Piet and Frans. He and his wife Joséphine gave us coffee and showed us an old photo of the farm after the First World War, when it was almost totally ruined. He also told us that his father and mother lived in the nearby village of Rosières, so after we said our goodbyes we decided to detour from the route taken by Piet and Frans, and go to meet the son of their former host.

François and Joséphine study Piet's book

Lihu farm after WWI

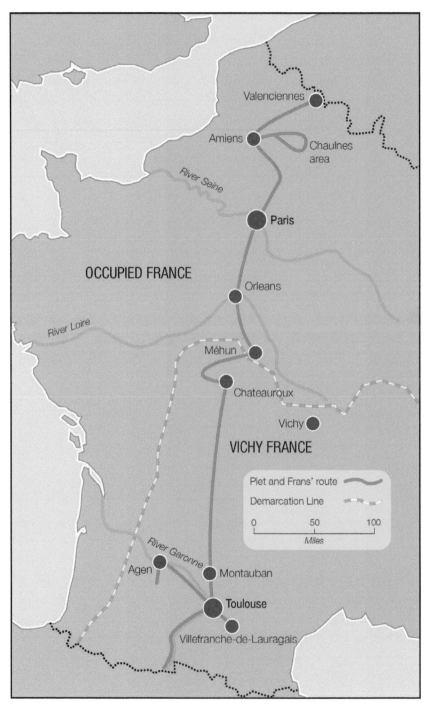

The route taken by Piet and Frans through France

On the way back to Lihons we passed the local cemetery, and went in to investigate. In the centre was a monument to the family ***Vanneufville***, which we decided must be the correct spelling of the name. When we reached his home in Rosières, M Vanneufville confirmed that it was correct. He was aged 11 in 1943, and remembered Dutchmen coming to the farm. His father had died in 1966, but he showed us a photo of his father's wedding.

Talking of Dutchmen, Piet has a few words to say about his use of the term:

Throughout this essay I have used the expression "Dutch" instead of Netherlands or Netherlander as this is generally understood in the English speaking world. But in wartime we objected to be called thus as it sounded like "Deutsch", which in our language means German. And that was one thing we did not like to be called.

In Rosières we found a restaurant which had been recommended by François, and had an excellent lunch. We then headed east to rejoin the route taken by Piet and Frans.

We left the hospitable Vanneuville family the next morning after another night between sheets. Although we were welcome to have stayed longer but they understood that we wanted to get on our way. On parting we were given provender for the day. With their good wishes for a safe journey we returned to Lihons the way we had come, aiming to find the Route Nationale 17 to try to get transport towards Paris. As Roye was also on this road we may have the opportunity to get help of some sort from the Dutch representative we had been told about.

Going south from Lihons along a country road to avoid Chaulnes we crossed over a railway bridge and to our consternation found going down on the other side on our left a large German airbase with planes and swarming with airmen. The perimeter, which ran along the road we walked on was patrolled with dogs and there were sentries at the entrance. But nobody took any notice of two backpackers as we passed on to the village of Chilly and via Fransart to Hattencourt.

Hattencourt

We headed through Chilly and Fransart in intermittent showers, but could see no sign of the former German airfield there. After leaving Fransart we soon found ourselves back in Hattencourt, our starting point that morning.

There we met Monsieur Herpoël, a farmer and coal and fuel merchant, whom we asked if we could find shelter for the night. He regretted that he could not have us to stay that night and took us to a widow, Madame Blondel (no, not the film star!⁵) to stay there for the night but were welcome the following day. That is where we returned to the next day and were put up in the loft over the horse's stable. He informed us that the Dutch Consulate in Roye was no longer there but he was in touch with "the other Side" and that regularly planes from England landed in the field behind his farm.

A rather dangerous statement to make to two perfect strangers! He made himself out to be a very important man in the "resistance". If we had some patience he would fix it for us to be flown to England by the next plane. Whatever his reasons were for spinning us these yarns was not quite clear, but we in our cynicism found him a braggart and neither of us was stupid enough to swallow it. Only three or four miles to the north was the strongly defended German airbase we had passed only a few days previously. Also would the British risk one of their valuable planes to pick up two unknown Dutch lads, who were of no importance, to take them to Britain from such a place? No way!

We lived well the four days we stayed at M and Mme Herpoël. We did various chores for them like cleaning vegetables, peeling potatoes and chopping firewood for the stove. We suspected M Herpoël's other business to be as black as his coal. There was a constant coming and going of "customers", many of them German servicemen. At first, when we spotted them coming up the drive, we dived into the empty horse-stable to hide under the straw. But soon we found out that the Germans were more interested in the butter, eggs and other produce obtainable than the two of us and we stopped hiding and carried on as usual.

Thursday 1 July was washing day, and just as we were hanging out on

---

5   We believe that the film star to whom Piet refers was Joan Blondell, an American actress who starred in various Hollywood films in the 1930s.

Old cobbler's shop in Hattencourt

the wire fence our wet washing to dry in the sun two Germans in the green uniforms with the gorgets of the dreaded "Grüne Feldpolizei" (Field police) appeared. With the speed of greased lightning the laundry was collected and we dived into the stable for the horse, who fortunately was not at home.

Perhaps Piet was being slightly harsh in his assessment of M Herpoël, who may have been exaggerating his role in the Resistance but could also have been playing a double game with the Germans. However, Piet and Frans were taking no chances.

We decided the next day that we had wasted enough time and would be leaving the next Monday. We spun a yarn about going to Roye to see the Consul's replacement.

Before leaving on the Monday morning we thanked our host and hostess profusely and marched out of the village. Just before the last houses I noticed a cobbler in his workshop and as our footwear had lost some of the metal studs and others were showing wear, I thought it wise to have it seen to. Entering his little bothy I explained our needs. He professed to have no studs available; I had however spotted on a shelf a cardboard box with German studs, similar to the ones on our boots. I took off one of my boots, plonked the box on his workbench and indicated him to get started. Removing my second boot I spoke to Frans in our own language to do the same and with both of us in stockinged feet watched the cobbler hammering at our footwear. He must, from our "put-on" guttural utterings have taken us for Germans. With the job finished and our boots back on our feet and expressing our satisfaction I asked him how much we owed him. He shook his head indicating that it was all right. With a "We are not beggars" and leaving a one hundred franc note on his bench we went out. To this day I am convinced that he was much relieved to be rid of his strange customers.

We had dropped our plan to go to the Route Nationale 17 and Roye and made our mind up, considering our good fortune and finances, to travel by train to Paris. We returned by a different route to Chaulnes via Fonches, thus bypassing the airfield. The Michelin map was a great help.

Next door to our *chambre d'hote* was a house with the name 'Herpoël' on the gate. We guessed that the owner might be a descendant of the family that sheltered Piet and Frans, and rang the bell twice, but there was no response. We were therefore unable to follow up this potential lead.

The following day we made a brief excursion from Hattencourt along the road to Fonches, in order to trace part of the route back to Chaulnes on foot. In Fonches there is a cemetery and war memorial with several mentions of the Blondel family, many of whom died in the First World War. On the way back into Hattencourt we met and chatted to an old man, who said he was the son of a cobbler and pointed out to us a house in the village where a cobbler used to work. It was impossible to be certain, but perhaps that was the workshop of the unfortunate fellow who encountered two assertive Dutchmen in 1943!

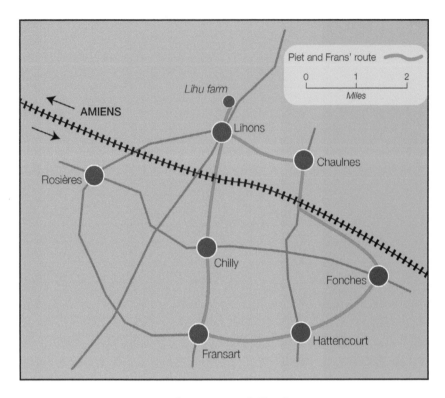

Wanderings around Chaulnes

Chapter 4

To Paris and Beyond

fter a week in rural France, Piet and Frans took the train to
Paris.

*At Chaulnes station we found that the direct train to Paris had already left,
but were advised that the next train would go to Paris via Amiens, where
we must change trains. It was a very fruitful journey; firstly there was
no inspection of tickets or passes; secondly in conversation with a young
Frenchman we learned how to travel furthest on French Railways for the
least expenditure. This appealed very much to our Dutch instincts (not
unlike those of the Scots!), and would be a boon to our financial situation.
The only drawback was that it worked only on the small local non-corridor
branch trains, where no identity and ticket check could be held.*

Having a Scottish wife, Piet was aware of that nation's reputation for
parsimony, but always maintained that the Dutch were equally careful of
their cash! We did not feel sufficiently adventurous to try to emulate his
method – our passion for research only reached so far, and not into falling
foul of the French authorities. Furthermore, the non-corridor trains no
longer run on the French railway system, and they seem to have tightened
up their security processes in the last 72 years.

*At Amiens we changed to an express train with the feared corridor coaches
and travelled non-stop to Paris, Gare du Nord, passing such well-known
places as Montdidier, Compiegne, Chantilly and Saint Denis. There was
no check which boosted our morale.*

We picked up our luggage in Hattencourt and returned to Chaulnes by bus, and also took the Paris train via Amiens, arriving as they did at the Gare du Nord.

Paris to Orléans

Standing outside this Paris main terminal station, we were overcome by the number of uniformed enemy servicemen milling around. Soon we realised they were just on leave in the capital and not in the least interested in two campers. Ignored by them we settled on a café terrasse and ordered two coffees. The surly waiter deposited two cups of a liquid, as black as my soul, in front of us. I ventured to ask for milk and sugar. But that was a mistake. The sullen reply was "Pas du lait" (no milk) and he pointed at a bottle of a clear liquid on the table and said: "Sucre", whereupon he disappeared to entertain some other hapless clients. It was possible that he mistook us for "boches"; so we forgave him. The coffee was some substitute, probably chicory or roasted acorns, and the "sugar" was a solution of saccharine and water. We did [spend] a very long time over our beverage, meantime counting our money.

Before leaving home in Holland I had sold my stamp collection for an exorbitant sum, the equivalent of £150 in Sterling; but this had now dwindled to the princely sum of £25 to see us all the way to the South of France; and who knows how far beyond. For an emergency I had my silver fork and spoon set; a 6th birthday present.

When paying our bill I enquired from the waiter where I could obtain Michelin maps and he pointed to one of the side streets. We left without leaving a tip.

The lady in the little stationer's shop, where we bought our map from Paris south to Orléans, was of a different disposition than the waiter. We had decided that with our acquired knowledge of how to diddle the French Railways we would try it and see how far we would get, and Orléans seemed a good target to aim for. She was very helpful in explaining to two innocents in Paris the station from which the train departed and how to get there by Metro; where we had to change once to reach Gare d'Austerlitz. Thanks to helpful passengers on the Metro we made the change at the correct intersection to reach Gare d'Austerlitz.

Gare du Nord

We also had coffee on the terrace of a café overlooking the Gare du Nord, though our waiter was much friendlier and more welcoming than Piet's (perhaps due to an expected tip). We had no success, however, in tracking down the nearby stationer's shop where they bought maps. Our finances were in much better shape than Piet's – due to the spread of ATMs and internationally accepted bank cards, cash was easily available to us whenever we needed it. Credit cards were unheard of in 1943.

Piet and Frans passed through Paris very quickly, anxious to press on south, but in our case it seemed a shame not to spend at least a day in the city. We went into 'sightseeing mode' and wandered around all day, exploring places we had not previously visited. The following morning we took the Metro to Gare d'Austerlitz; like Piet, we were glad of the help of fellow travellers when our case got trapped in the remorseless jaws of an entrance barrier. Kind hands helped to wrench the jaws open and rescue our luggage. From the station we took the train to Orléans (though we paid for our tickets).

At this station we would try out the cheap way of travelling. I left Frans guarding our rucksacks in the middle of the large booking hall. Not in some dark corner but right in view of everybody. We were of the opinion that would rouse the least suspicion. After consulting our map, which had different symbols for the different types of stations and halts, I bought two singles to the nearest station from the one we were leaving; checked the timetable for the time and platform of departure. Also from our map found the last little halt from Orléans, Fleury les-Aubrais, which we must not miss.

We could not stay in the booking hall all the time until the train left. Thus we went to look for a seat at the platform. As it was a terminal station all the platforms were gated. So we went to our platform but the ticket inspector would not let us through until the train had drawn in. We discussed this in Dutch with each other, whereupon the ticket collector pointed to entrance one. That is where we made for. There was no check so we went through and found a row of benches against the windowed wall of what looked like an office. We sat there for a while doing nothing till I thought to buy a newspaper at the kiosk in the booking hall. Out I went and came back with "Die Völkische Beobachter", a German paper in both French and German. At least Frans could read the German bit so we divided the paper in two.

The part of the platform concourse where we were ensconced was quite deserted apart from German servicemen passing in front of us, disappearing into a doorway to our left and later coming out again. They paid no attention to us and we reciprocated by not noticing them.

There appeared a "flic", Paris policeman, and asked for our papers. We produced our Dutch identity cards, with portrait and fingerprint together with a homemade German stamp, with eagle and swastika. These satisfied him and he went on his way, swinging his truncheon.

Sometime later we were asked again for our papers; this time by a railway employee, judging by the uniform. He was not so easily satisfied and started shouting at us that we could not sit there and had to go back to the booking hall to wait for the arrival of our train.

But who should come to our aid? Our friend the flic. An argument between the two ensued, of which there was much that I could not follow; arms were swinging and fingers were pointed at something above our heads. The upshot of it all was that we could stay where we were. And tranquillity returned. Curious, I stood up to see at what fingers had been pointed and discovered that on the wall above the windows was a long noticeboard "Auskunfstelle für Deutsche Wehrmachts Angehörigen" (Information bureau for German Services). Once again we had been taken for Germans.

Our "papers" at the time consisted of "doctored" identity cards and Youth hostel membership cards, both in the Dutch language and looking quite official. They had been embellished with a faked German official stamp with eagle and swastika.

To obtain such a stamp one had to either purloin one from a German office, but a less risky way was to obtain a fresh imprint made with a newly inked stamp-pad in the violet colour loved by German officialdom. Such a stamp may appear on an envelope passed by the censor. With the aid of a freshly peeled hardboiled egg this impression can now be transferred to any form.

Eventually our train arrived at the platform. We boarded as did all the other passengers and as we set off we passed "our flic" with a wave.

When the train reached its first small halt we paid special attention to the working of such a halt, at the arrival and departure of a train. The first thing we noticed was the absence of a platform and passengers climbed in and out by means of running boards along the carriages. The whole station operation rested in the hands of one man, or woman, who had to close the gates on the arrival of the train, collect the tickets at one end, and wave the train off when all doors are closed.

Once again Piet describes the help they were given by French people and the camaraderie and solidarity they expressed, united against the Germans.

Soon after leaving Paris we came into conversation with our fellow passengers who, after finding out that we were "Hollandais" and not "Boches", became very friendly, as we were in the same boat. Again the goodies came our way. Fresh bread, butter wrapped in vine leaves, eggs and on one occasion two round wooden boxes with cheese. One Frenchman informed me that he worked as a chef in the kitchen of a German officers' mess in Paris, was now on leave, and passed on to us a bundle of German ration cards which could be used anywhere in occupied territory and were valid for an indefinite period. If we could not use them all they were worth money!

We also noticed that we were not the only ones who were into the secret of cheap rail travel. At many of the small halts and stations we saw the process in action. Wait till the train slowly chugs away from the halt and while the railway person is busy taking in the tickets, throw out the luggage from the still slow moving train, and jump after it at the far end of the halt and disappear from the unfenced precinct.

At Fleury-les-Aubrais, the last halt before the main station of Orléans, we did our trick with a variant: first Frans went out, then the rucksacks and instruments, and while number two jumped out the other had already collected our stuff. How the French railways in wartime made a profit remains a puzzle.

We took the train direct to Orléans and checked into a hotel near the station. After leaving the luggage, we returned to the station and bought tickets back up the line to Fleury, with the intention of walking back to Orléans from the place where Piet and Frans jumped train.

After a day of bizarre experiences we sought and found a place to rest our heads for the night with an Italian family. How to find an evening meal and a place to pass the night, as we learned by chance at Lihu: ask for water, get wine, can't pay, entertain and be invited to stay. It worked many times.

When morning broke we set off on foot towards the centre of Orléans and the railway station to try our trick again. It was a straight road from Fleury to the town and we passed a very high wall and wondered what was behind it. The answer came when we came to a side street and saw the entrance gate of Orléans prison. We continued to the railway station leaving the prison behind us.

From Fleury we set off on foot back towards Orléans, a distance of two or three miles. We came to a long high wall and wondered if it was the one Piet mentions. However, on the other side was a large cemetery, including a section with many graves from the First World War, set out in serried ranks. There were a number of Jewish graves, and a few Muslim burials.

Further on was another high wall, with a building inside which had barred windows. We walked round and found an entrance gate, closed and locked, with no sign of what the place was, though we guessed it

Orléans prison

was the prison. A quick Google later confirmed it was in fact Orléans prison, closed only in September 2014, and awaiting a decision about its future fate. We spent the night in Orléans, and saw its gothic cathedral and large equestrian statue of Joan of Arc, though our spirits were slightly dampened by the pouring rain.

The Demarcation Line

At the station I left Frans again in the booking hall with our possessions to consult the timetable and buy the tickets. We were aiming this time for Vierzon to cross there the "Ligne de Démarcation" into Vichy France, and to jump train at Theillay.

Turning away from the ticket window I noticed Frans in conversation with two gents in civilian clothes and making frantic gestures to me. I was not perturbed as I knew Frans had very little French, although he began to pick it up. He relied on me to do the talking.

When I joined them I could not help noticing that the two "gentlemen" were wearing the swastika-badges of the "Reichssicherheitsdienst" (State security service) on their lapels.

In an aside, Piet explains how he acquired his language skills.

I had been fortunate with my languages. After WW1, when I was a very young child, an orphan came to my home in Zaandam. She would have been about fifteen years of age. She was dressed in rags and asked (just as Frans and I did) for a place to sleep and also for work. She turned out to be a "Volksdeutsche" (German national) who had been ousted from Hungary and had trekked all that way to Holland. My mother decided to keep her and she was given the maid's room. And that is how when I came down the following morning I found a strange lady at breakfast. Later that day she was taken to shop for new clothes and a medical. Hilda could not speak any Dutch nor could my mother German. As a toddler I became messenger between both. That was my grounding in German. Later at Grammar school I had to learn three foreign languages, and was taught the correct grammar. This is to explain how [my German] came to [stand me in] good stead in later life. (Hilda stayed with us for 9 years until she married a local Dutchman)

The story of the German maid is interesting. The Netherlands was neutral in the First World War and did not suffer occupation by the Germans then. Dutch people therefore would be more sympathetic to a German refugee at that time, compared with the situation after World War II.

The two "gents" were surprised to be addressed in their own tongue and wanted to know what we as "Holländer" were doing in the middle of France. I explained that we were Dutch volunteers working on the Atlantic Defence System and that after three months' work we had been given ten days leave. "Why were we then not going home, to Holland?" "Because we now have the opportunity to see something of France and we were are going around the countryside as "Wanderburschen" (backpackers)". That satisfied them and, after a cursory look at our "Ausweisen" (papers, with egg-stamp), we parted with handshakes and a "Gute Reise" off to our train. I still do not know where I got it from to produce a story like that. But it proves that a "Dumme Holländer" (stupid Dutchman) is not necessarily more stupid than two Germans. Volunteers got indeed leave; forced labourers not. I knew that but they didn't.

We took our seats in the train to travel to Vierzon and then started trembling; the after effect from our narrow escape at the station. Then we intended to wash the dust of occupied France from our feet and enter what we thought was unoccupied Vichy France.

Piet was good at thinking on his feet and spinning a plausible yarn, though doubtless his excellent German was a bonus. The sentence *'I knew that but they didn't'* is strange. Piet claimed to be a volunteer; if the Germans did not know that volunteers got leave, why would they believe him?

A divided France

After the French surrender to the Germans in 1940, the country was divided into two parts: the north plus the Atlantic coast became occupied France, under the direct rule of the Nazis, and the rest was unoccupied or 'Vichy' France, after the name of the town where the government was located. In practice the Vichy authorities collaborated with the Nazis, but the area was free of direct German surveillance and relatively easier for escapers to move through.

In November 1942, however, following Allied landings in North Africa, the Nazis moved to occupy the whole of France, although their control over the previously 'unoccupied' area increased only gradually. Therefore, when Piet says *'what we thought was unoccupied Vichy France'*, this implies that he and Frans had not realised about the takeover in November 1942 and thought there was no German presence in the south. In any case, there was still a 'Demarcation Line' between the two halves of France which was guarded and had to be crossed.

On the Michelin map this place [Vierzon] looked as likely a place for crossing the Demarcation Line as any. As usual we entered in conversation with the people in our compartment as soon as they knew of our antecedents. When we made it clear that we intended to cross at Vierzon into unoccupied France eyebrows were lifted, heads were shaken and it was argued that a far better place to do that would be Méhun, a little further along the line. But, I explained, we did not have tickets to that place. "No problem" declared a fellow traveller; he lived in Méhun and would get us out of the station bypassing the ticket collector. We passed the halt at Theillay, where we had intended to "jump", passed Vierzon and arrived at Méhun station. There our guide led us through a room, a passage and we left the station via a side entrance, in our case "exit". Maybe our friendly Frenchman didn't have a ticket either. Before parting he pointed to a bakery shop, where at that time of the morning a queue of women was waiting for bread. He told us that in that shop they were "good people" who would help us, as they were of the "Resistance".

From Orléans we took the train to Vierzon, and there hired a car. We drove to Méhun-sur-Yevre and found the station. The next task was to track down the bakery. We ambled down the road to the town centre, spotted a bakery on a corner, and went in to enquire. The woman in the shop said that the bakery was relatively new, but there was an older one just down the road, which was now closed. We found the shop she mentioned, which seemed to be in a plausible location, between the station and the town, to be the one Piet mentions.

Later we visited the Resistance Museum in the city of Bourges, and there found evidence that there was a baker named Camille Chevalier in Méhun, who was prominent in the Resistance. His shop was in the Rue Jeanne d'Arc, the main street of Méhun, as was the old bakery we saw.

We joined the end of the unorderly queue and when our turn came I asked the lady serving for a word in private. We were led into a room behind

the shop. There I explained who we were and what our intentions were. She told us at large about the situation at the frontier line which ran along the river Cher, some three miles to the west. There was a bridge over the river at the end of an almost straight road with a German sentry box from which the last stretch of our approach could be observed. The sentry box was not always, or constantly, manned as most of "les boches" had been sent to fight in Russia.

Méhun station

The bridge of Cher

Her little daughter, aged between 10 and 12, would go on the "biciclette" and reconnoitre the road and bridge. Then come back along the road we were walking and give us a signal if all was clear. In the other case she would lead us via a side road north to a, at that time of the year, fordable place out of sight of the bridge.

The German guard post during WW2

We went our way and after a time the little girl on her bike overtook us. On her return from the bridge she gave us the "all clear" signal. We crossed the bridge with its empty sentry box and entered the village of Quincey.

The road west from the station led straight as a die over flat fields filled with sunflowers and wind turbines. We walked on the left, facing the oncoming traffic, and finally came to the river Cher and its bridge. No sentry box. We crossed the bridge, with no sign that once this was part of a line which once divided France in two, and like Piet, we entered the village of Quincy.

Chapter 5

Vichy France

Piet tells what happened after he and Frans crossed the Demarcation Line.

A halt was made on the far side of the village in a field behind a hedge to brew a celebratory cuppa, which we drank the Dutch way without milk. Bread was buttered and we opened one of our round boxes of cheese. But we found that the centre had gone bad; it was swarming with very tiny minute white worms. Not to waste it all we spooned the centre out and ate only the outer crust. The second box underwent the same treatment. It was not much to our liking. Very much later we learned that we had thrown away the best part and should have discarded the mouldy crust!

We stopped a farmer, driving a car with a trailer, and in my now improved vernacular French asked: "On peut monter?" (May we have a lift). "Oui, get in the trailer". This was already occupied by a very large sow, who strongly objected to our intrusion. Constantly fighting off the attentions of the angry swine we reached the village of Reuilly, far enough from the line dividing France in two parts. We had received information that Dutch farmers had settled there after the Great War of 1914-18. We had no luck finding any settlers, but were kindly received by a labourer, his wife and young family. He had leased from the Council the right to make hay on a stretch of the road to feed through the winter his only cow and we helped him to tend the hay. We could not stay for longer than one night, otherwise we would have helped him bringing in the hay a few days later.

Next morning we were on the road again. This time to Massay. Frans is not feeling very well. Could it have been that cheese? I dread the

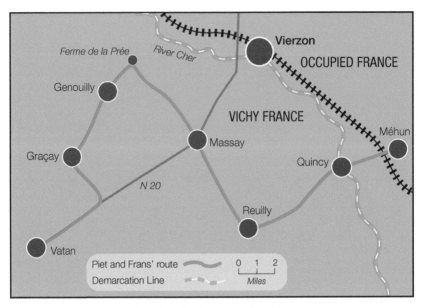

Crossing the Demarcaction Line

situation where one of us is too ill to continue and ponder what to do in such a case.

On reaching Quincy we had drinks in a little café and bought food at a *boulangerie* for a picnic next to a fishing lake. After lunch we walked back to Méhun and our hire car. Driving back over the Cher we passed through Quincy and went on to Reuilly. We got little information at the tourist office there, but did manage to buy a bottle of red wine from a *cave*.

The farm De la Prée

It was reported there lived a Dutch farmer and his family on a farm called "De la Pree". When we came to the farm the Dutch farmer turned out to be Swiss. It is possible that the French are not aware of the difference between these nationalities.

We were very well received by this very large family who welcomed us at their table and found us a space to spread our sleeping bags. They also provided Frans with some medicine for his stomach upset and he soon felt much better.

The following morning we drove back through Reuilly and on to Massay, where we enquired at the *mairie*, but the farm 'De la Prée' was unknown. We next asked at a bar; people there had not heard of the farm, but guessed that it must be close to the village of Saint Georges sur la Prée. This was not in the direction we expected, but we had no other clues, so off we went. On the way we spotted a postman making deliveries, so stopped to ask him – thinking that if anyone would know where the farm was, he would. However, we were disappointed.

We pressed on into Saint Georges and went to the *mairie*. The kind lady there said she thought she knew where the farm was, though it was now abandoned. She made a number of phone calls to colleagues in other offices, and announced she was now confident of its location. She marked it on our map, close to a large chateau called 'Maison Fort'. We thanked her profusely and headed out. In the square there was a poster about the Demarcation Line, and while we were studying that another lady emerged from the *mairie* and said there was an old couple across the road who knew the area well and could help us.

She introduced us to them, and they invited us in and chatted to us for a while. They confirmed the location of the farm, and that it had been run by a Swiss farmer during the war, and had been a centre for the Resistance in the area.

Finding the farm was harder than expected; we drove along the indicated road, but the only farm was clearly still in operation. Baffled, we stopped there to enquire. The farmer told us it was back down the road, right next to 'Maison Fort', but up a long drive (and so hidden from the road). There was in fact a gate marked '*Défense d'entrée*' (no entry). Ignoring the sign, we walked up the tree-lined drive, and there it was – the farm 'De la Prée', with several buildings surrounding a grassy space, and thick woods hiding it from view. It seemed to be a perfect place for Resistance activities.

The place was deserted, but clearly still in good condition and possibly used occasionally for one purpose or another. In one of the barns an old car was parked. We returned to our hire car, elated at having found another of the places where Piet and Frans stayed on their odyssey.

Entrance to farm 'De la Prée'

Farm 'De la Prée'

The head of this lovely household advised us to go to the nearby Mairie at Genouilly to inquire about the existence of any farmers from Holland living in the area. At the Mairie we were looked at with suspicion; they did not know of any and could not help us any further. Quickly we left this inhospitable office and went on to Graçay.

Luck will have it that on our way there we met three Dutch seminarists who lived in, and studied at, the monastery "Les Gaudirons" nearby. They were out for a stroll and were pleased to meet some fellow countrymen, and for the first time we conversed in our mother tongue. They knew of no Dutch people living in the vicinity but had some very good information for us.

Far to the south, in Montauban in the Departement Tarn-et-Garonne, they informed us was the "Office Neerlandaise", formerly the Dutch Consulate, where state pensions were paid out to Dutch emigrés living there. The Consulate had been closed since the diplomatic relations between the Dutch Government in exile in Britain and that of Vichy France had been broken off.

This was some real good information at last after all our wandering about searching for kinfolk to obtain such [news]. The big question was how to get to Montauban, hundreds of miles to the south. There was an express train service from Chateauroux, the nearest mainline station south, but our exchequer could not fund such a journey and we knew not of any branch trains.

The solution seemed to be to take to the road. Our Michelin map told us there was the Route Nationale 20, going all the way there and even further to Toulouse and on to Andorra. The prospects were legion. We stayed that night with a Flemish farmer's family, and it was a pleasure for the second time that day to converse in our own languages which are so similar.

An unsolved mystery

We had made up our minds to make for Montauban; after all, it was only 235 miles in a direct line. Mulling this over again as we set off towards the N20 we passed "Les Gaudirons", but saw nothing of our Dutch seminarists. Instead we were stopped by two gendarmes on bikes, who wanted to see our papers. They could make neither head nor tail of them and instructed us to report to the Gendarmerie in Vatan to have them checked. Then they mounted their bicycles and went on their way. The prospect of having our papers inspected at the police station did not sound too good to us. The risk of being found out was too great. We therefore continued on our way and reached the N20 four miles north of Vatan and its Gendarmerie.

This passage raises a problem which we frustratingly could not solve. Piet's story has proved to be strikingly accurate, and we have been able to track down a lot of the people and places he mentions. But of 'Les Gaudirons' we could find no trace. We went to Graçay and asked in the tourist office, but no-one there had heard of it. We sat in a bar in the main square, and even found an Englishman who had lived in the town for 20 years. He asked all the others in the bar, and there was total bafflement all round.

On the outskirts of Graçay at St Outrille is an old church with a twisted spire. We hypothesised that the seminary might have been associated with that, but there was no indication of accommodation linked to the church. Nearby was an abandoned farm, which could have been where Piet and Frans stayed, but there was no way of telling. We walked from Massay down the road towards the N20, but nowhere was there a sign of any building which once might have been a seminary.

'Gaudirons' is the French version of the Latin *'gaudeamus'* (let us rejoice), and we thought it possible that it was a temporary set-up for the war years only, and had long since disappeared. Back in England, we emailed the archives for the Catholic diocese of Bourges, hoping they might have records of the seminary. The helpful archivist informed us that the only seminary at that time was at Neuvy-sur-Barangeon, several miles away on the other side of Vierzon. It operated from 1937 to 1950 and did train some Dutch priests, but the geography could not be reconciled with Piet's account. Students based at Neuvy could not have been out for a stroll near Graçay; Piet and Frans would not have passed the seminary on the way from Graçay to the N20.

Clutching at straws, we surmised that the seminarists that Piet and Frans met might have been on a local placement at St Outrille, and that 'Les Gaudirons' was their nickname for the church or where they were staying. The theory may be far-fetched, but we still cannot think of a better. It is very frustrating.

Church of St Outrille, Graçay

Unexpected generosity

Luck was with us as almost immediately a canvas topped lorry stopped and took us on board. They were going to an army camp 6½ kilometres south of that city to deliver a load of underwear. We were delighted to learn this and sheltered by the canvas we went on our way and before reaching Vatan we overtook our two gendarmes on their bikes. Needless to say we did not wave to them!

South of Vatan the lorry stopped to let us off and turned into a side road. We were soon picked up by an open lorry with two men in the cab and one standing in the open back. There were a number of beehives in it as well. There was a sweet smell of honey even when we moved at speed and also some drowsy bees. We got in conversation with our companion on the back and told him that we were on our way to Montauban, to our consul there to see what help he could give us. We had no money for the train fare and therefore begged lifts. This resulted in him banging on the cabin roof, and we came to a stop along the dead straight road. And there and then a conference was held by the three men in such rapid French that I could not even guess the gist of it. We were also asked some questions, wanted to show our papers but that was not necessary.

The result of all this was that we were told that they would take us to the railway station at Chateauroux and leave us there in the waiting room. There we would wait for their return with something to eat on our journey. In the waiting room we were wondering whether they would indeed come back and if so, would they bring the police with them. But all was well. They did turn up with two food parcels and a bottle of wine "for the journey!". To crown it all they presented us with two railway tickets for the night express to Montauban, told us the time and platform of departure and not to worry about the Gendarmerie in Vatan as it would take a very long time to get the alert out over the Departement and by then we would be well outside it. We were so overcome that before we had a chance to properly express our gratitude they had gone.

Another brilliant example of the kindness of ordinary French people to two foreign refugees! But their reception in Montauban was less welcoming.

We had a catnap in the deserted waiting room, which towards departure time began to fill up. Once ensconced in the train on comfortable seats, in the compartment which had come from Orléans and was to go on to Toulouse, we fell into a fitful sleep, afraid to overrun our destination; but not to worry, our fellow travellers would warn us in time. The train sped southwards, passing (and maybe even stopping at) Limoges, Cahors and Brive till we reached Montauban, five Departements south, at about seven the next morning. Far too early to present ourselves at the office, which we found without any difficulty by asking the few people abroad at that time of day. We waited, sitting on a low wall, for the office to open and in the meantime having breakfast on the food provided by our kind benefactors.

Shortly before nine a gent arrived on a bicycle, which he parked in

Montauban

an archway, undid his trouser clips, noticed us and asked if we came to see him. He led us into a paper-strewn office and asked what he could do for us and received a terrible shock when we told him the reason for our visit. His first reaction was that we did best to return back to Holland as we did not know how dangerous it was here. We told him that it was not so safe in Holland either with all the German soldiery about and Allied airplanes dropping bombs all over the place. Landing in a concentration camp was also not our idea of a picnic. Furthermore having come this far we were determined not to go back but carry on, with or without whatever assistance he could provide. After all, he was the former Dutch Consul whose duty it was to help nationals in difficulty abroad.

After having taken in all that, his attitude changed a little and he told us that in Toulouse there was someone who could possibly be of help to us. His name was Aarts (Dutch sounding, but could be Flemish) who had an office in the building of the "Banque Franco-Belge" in the Rue Vélane 6. We said that we would go and see him but we had no money for the fare to Toulouse. We received from him each a one hundred franc note and left. I am convinced that he thought that was a cheap price to pay to get rid of us.

Piet and Frans had more help from ordinary people than from those who had an official duty to care for them.

From Graçay we drove back to Vierzon and left the car, and then took the train to Chateauroux, changing there to travel south to Montauban. We arrived late in the afternoon, and dragged our case over cobbled streets from the station to our hotel in the city centre, about a kilometre. Montauban is an attractive city, but we had limited time for sightseeing. We had no success in finding the location of the ex-consul's office, despite asking at the tourist office and looking round the streets near the station for a likely building. So it was on to Toulouse.

Chapter 6

Toulouse and the South

Piet writes about their arrival in Toulouse:

At around half past eleven that same day we arrived at Toulouse station. Our fear of travelling in corridor trains in Vichy France had vanished since we left Chateauroux, as since then we had travelled with valid tickets and there was no check by the Germans as yet in the unoccupied part of France.

Without difficulty we found the Rue Vélane and at no.6 we entered the bank, asked for Monsieur Aarts and were shown a side door leading to a staircase at the top of which we found Mijnheer Aarts in his office. He was indeed a Dutchman and listened to our story. He informed us that regularly small groups of Dutch escapers were being helped across the Pyrenees to Spain by "passeurs" (guides) from the "Résistance", the French underground movement; but it would cost money. Explaining we hadn't any to speak of, he said that he would see what could be arranged about that. His matter of fact way boosted our confidence in him; more so than the tales we had heard from M Herpoël earlier. But first he had to find accommodation for us whilst we were in Toulouse. Picking up the telephone he spoke to someone in rapid French, and after a while, whilst we recounted briefly our adventures since leaving Holland, Joop van Dam, another Dutch escaper with an excellent command of French, turned up. He took us to the apartment of Madame Boutonnet, a red-haired widow of an orchestra violinist, who had been killed. We had to stay indoors and not to show ourselves to the world outside.

On arriving in Toulouse, our first visit was to the Resistance Museum in the south of the city. We spoke with Sophie, whom we had earlier emailed, but she was unable to give us much help, and had no record at all of M Aarts, although he was clearly prominent in helping escapers cross the Pyrenees. The museum had two floors of exhibits, though many of them were about the return of local people from concentration and forced labour camps after the war. There was some information about those who crossed the Pyrenees to Spain, including a plan of Miranda de Ebro concentration camp, where many (including Piet) were interned[6].

On our way back to the city centre we visited the Rue Vélane and found number 6, the office of M Aarts who was so helpful to Piet and Frans and other escapers from the Nazis. It is sad that we were unable to find any mention of him in our researches, although Piet says later that he was shot by the Germans for his activities.

Toulouse is an attractive and important city, but for Piet and Frans it was more of a transportation centre for their excursions to various parts of the South.

No. 6 Rue Vélane

---

6   Piet's stay in Miranda de Ebro is described in Chapter 12.

A frosty reception

On Tuesday 13 July Mr. Aarts called us to his office and told us that we could no longer stay with Madame Boutonnet, and that it would be best if we could find accommodation somewhere in the countryside, at some farm or so, as it could be some time before he could arrange a party large enough to be worth taking across the mountains. Then, after we had found such a place, we would write and let him have our address so that when the opportunity came he could call us back to Toulouse. He provided us with the address and name of a "Dutch" village priest, Monseigneur van Breukelen, in a place called Mourville-Hautes in the hills above Villefranche-de-Lauragais, some 20 miles to the southeast of Toulouse. We left his office rather disappointed.

We packed our bags, said "Au revoir" to the red-haired widow, and went by train to Villefranche. From the station we took the road to Mourville, climbing steadily into the hills of Haute Garonne and the Languedoc until we reached the hamlet. The only building of any size was the presbytery where Monseigneur van Breukelen turned out to be a Flemish-speaking Belgian. He received us on the steps and kept on shaking his head so much that I expected it any moment to roll [off], telling us that it was not possible to find a place to sleep for us, not even for one night, and that we did best to return to our homes. (As if these were just around the corner!) It was far too dangerous around here. That story we had heard before and could not imagine a more peaceful and secure place than that lonely spot in the hills. He saw us off with the pronouncement "That he would pray for us". He didn't even know our names!

The day after our arrival in Toulouse we also took the train to Villefranche-de-Lauragais. We did not think we would be able to walk to Mourville-Hautes and get back in time for the last train, so we called for a taxi to take us up to the village. The driver was clearly baffled as to why we would want to go to such a remote place.

The village is perched on top of a low hill. It is dominated by the church, but it was not clear which building was the presbytery. We walked round the side of the church and found a cemetery overlooking the surrounding countryside. Back at the church one or two people had assembled for an event, and they showed us where the presbytery was. We took care to photograph the actual door where Piet and Frans were turned away.

Mourville-Hautes church

Somewhat dejected we retraced our steps downhill to the valley below and Villefranche. Arriving there we found the station locked up and in darkness with no train back to Toulouse, where we would have no place for the night. We looked for somewhere to pass the night and found parked in a siding a row of goods vans. We found one that was unlocked and on the wooden floor spread our sleeping bags to await the dawn. We daren't sleep in case railway staff turned up early and found us there. It was very cold that night so we were glad when the first light came.

We walked back to Villefranche, as Piet and Frans did. Our route took us through the nearby villages of Rieumajou, Folcarde, and St Assiscle (the latter with an impressive church). We took a train back to Toulouse, and did not have to spend the night in a goods wagon. However, behind the station at Villefranche we found an overgrown siding, which may well have been the place where the wagons were parked, back in 1943.

The presbytery where Piet and Frans were turned away

French countryside near Mourville-Hautes

Off to Agen

Without making our usual toilet I bought tickets back to Toulouse and Mr. Aarts to tell him about the fiasco at the address he had given us. Van Dam was called into the office again to discuss the situation. A solution to the impasse was found: that van Dam, with his much better command of French, should come with us and find somewhere for us to stay. Then return to Toulouse to inform Mr. Aarts of our whereabouts.

So the same day, the three of us went by train northwest to Agen in the Lot-et-Garonne to look for a Father Wouterlood, a Dutch priest, who we found eventually in the "Secours Nationale", a soup kitchen for down-and-outs. Here we were given a meal. Afterwards we were directed to a seminary on the outskirts of town where we were given a bed for the night in their guestrooms.

By now we were becoming quite familiar with Toulouse railway station and its chaotic ticket office. We travelled next to Agen, as Piet and Frans had done 72 years before. Agen itself is a very pleasant town on the banks of the Garonne (the Garonne river features quite a lot in Piet's story) and close to the Canal du Midi. It has an attractive pedestrianised shopping street and a large number of old buildings.

Staff in the Catholic diocesan office in Agen were very helpful, and dug out their records of Father Wouterlood. He was ordained priest in 1942, worked at the 'église des Jacobins' (Jacobins' church) in Agen, and died suddenly in 1962. We found the church, a beautiful and impressive structure near the town centre, but now converted to an art gallery and exhibition space. We went in, and were uninspired by the current exhibition, but the vaulted ceilings and light and airy feeling of the place were worth the admission price.

The main seminary in Agen in those days was also easy to find, on the southern outskirts of town. It is now called the John XXIII Centre, and is a massive building used for various purposes. So far we felt that we had tracked Piet and Frans quite well during their stay in Agen – the next stage was to follow them into the country south of the town. Public transport did not meet our needs, so we hired a car in order to continue the pursuit.

Centre Jean XIII, Agen

Jacobins' Church, Agen

After a good night's rest we set off on the road again and found in Moirax, Pierre Driemans, who with his knowledge of the area came with us to help us find a place to stay; preferably together. In this we were not successful, but found in Leyrac a farmer by the name of Warmoeskerk, a Dutchman, who engaged Frans – probably he looked the younger and sturdier of the two of us – but would only take him alone.

We left Frans with Warmoeskerk while Joop and I, after Driemans left us to return home, continued our search. We found in the hamlet of Fals the Standaert family, father, mother and their younger son. They originated from Flanders and could still speak Flemish with an accent.

Churchyard at Fals

They were willing to take me on; the pay would be three hundred francs per month with food and lodging. Four hours free per week, either on Saturday afternoon or Sunday morning.

Their married son lived with his wife on an adjacent farm of their own, at no great distance.

In the meantime Frans had discovered that farmer Warmoeskerk intended to report his presence on the farm to the police in Agen. So he packed his bags and found us at the Standaert's farm. Standaert's son is prepared to take Frans, on the same conditions as those agreed for me. So now we are, although not at the same place, close together on adjoining farms. Near enough for contact and mutual comfort.

On Saturday 17 July I went with Joop van Dam to the railway station at Astaffort for his return to Toulouse and to inform Mr. Aarts of our addresses.

I return into the hills to Fals, on the way passing by Frans to tell him of the arrangements. We now settle down to do our jobs on the farm(s).

We drove south from Agen and reached the tiny and sleepy hilltop village of Fals. The little *mairie* was closed, and we struggled to find anyone to ask about the Standaert farm. Eventually we found the church, and wandered round the graveyard looking in vain for any family names. Then a lady arrived with flowers for the church, and was able to direct us to the farm – south from the village, down the hill, and just past the woods. We went back to the car and drove on, eager to see the farm where Piet spent so much time.

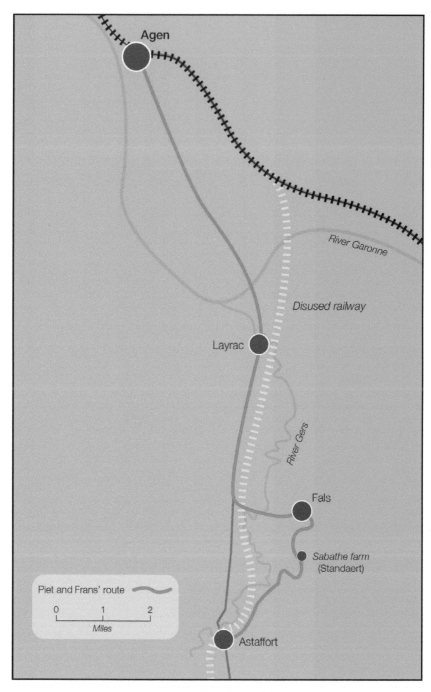

Agen

River Garonne

Disused railway

Layrac

River Gers

Fals

Sabathe farm
(Standaert)

Piet and Frans' route

0   1   2
Miles

Astaffort

Agen, Fals and Astaffort

Chapter 7

Rural Interlude

Piet spent two months working on the farm in Fals. He gives a fascinating description of life as a farmhand in rural southern France in 1943. As it is not something we could experience (nor would wish to!) we include it here without comment.

Life as a farmhand on a hill croft in Southern France was not a sinecure, as we soon found out. We were not used to the hard physical work, nor the long hours of work in the summer.

The farmhouse was small; the living room with the vast open hearth was also the place where the food was prepared and cooked on an open fire of bundles of twigs and sticks. The absence of a sink was of no matter as there was no drainage. Slops were thrown out through the door. Ideal for laying the dust! Sanitary arrangements were non-existent. A place in the shrubbery was all there was. The flies took care of the disposal. Toilet paper was an unheard-of luxury, but there was a shrub with very soft strong leaves, appropriately called Lavetera. No progress to gracious living had been made since the middle ages.

Off the living room was the bedroom for the elderly farmer and his wife, a prematurely old woman, wrinkled with dirt-ingrained skin and hands. There was no water for personal cleanliness.

The other downstairs room was a storeroom with a tiny barred windowless aperture. Their younger son and I had our "beds" there. From its ceiling beams hung flitches of bacon and other provisions in pillowcases to keep them from the rodents. They contained such stores as peas, beans, flower, grains and also a linen sack with candied sugar lumps. The mattress on my sleeping place had previously been used by someone with an incontinence problem and I thanked heaven for my groundsheet and sleeping bag.

The earthen floors of the dwelling were treated with animal blood; the exception was the enormous hearth which was paved with terra cotta tiles. There being no stairs the access to the first floor was by means of an outside ladder. This first floor, under the roof, was the storage space for the farm produce. It was also a haven for mice and fleas in incalculable numbers. There was no gas, electricity or piped water. Light was provided by candles and oil lamps. Water was stored in a large wine barrel on a two-wheeled cart parked in the shadow of a tree outside the only door to the premises. It was only used for food preparation, cooking, some washing (not too much) but not for personal hygiene or drinking. Not likely!

When the barrel became nearly empty it was drained into buckets and saved for the animals. To obtain a fresh supply an ox was yoked and harnessed to the cart and the trek to the spring higher up in the hills was made. This was a job allocated to me. Only one ox could be used because of the narrowness of the track. Reaching the spring where the clear cool water came out of the rock wall into a natural basin whose overflow ran down the track, the ox-drawn cart had to be turned to face downhill with the barrel still empty. How this was done will become clear when the story of how to work with a pair of oxen unfolds.

Once the ox is facing downhill the cart has to be immobilised with boulders in front and behind the wheels – just in case the animal spots a nice bit of greenery and starts making towards it. Now to unship the water pump. The inlet hose is put in the basin and the filling hose in the bung hole. The barrel must first be flushed out to get rid of any sediment before filling can begin. When full to overflowing the bung is replaced; the pump shipped; boulders removed and the journey home can be made. This was one of the easier tasks and also the most pleasant as one was away from the ever watchful eyes of "la patronne".

Oxen, who were used for all the heavy work on the farm like ploughing and harrowing the stony soil, worked in pairs. They were yoked together by the head with leather thongs so that their heads became as one. The yoke was fastened, usually by chain, to the appliance. The lefthand ox had the rein tied to its left ear and the other end was tied to the right ear of the other ox. Oxen, who are very strong, have only two speeds: dead slow and stop. To set them moving one holds a long stick with a sharpened nail at one end. With that they have to be prodded constantly in their rear quarters. No prod, no progress.

The prod was also used to steer and make a turn. To make a turn, let's say to the right, pull hard on the right rein. That ox will stop (he is not stupid). Prod with the nailed stick the backside of the lefthand ox; he will move (he's not stupid either). When the team is pointing in the right direction, start prodding the right hand ox. This way one can turn a cart with a span of oxen on the proverbial sixpence. Easy when you know how. But what our RSPCA would think of it I wouldn't know.

Being a big softy, I did find out a way with less hurt and cruelty. When making a noise (singing, shouting or such) behind the span they have the idea in their heads that there is someone behind them (remember they cannot turn their heads) with a sharp nail on a stick and to get away they'll move; not fast but move just the same. Stop making a noise and they stop. To make a turn one only needs to touch the already tender bottom of the one with the blunt end of the stick and he'll move. Now the other thinks that his ear is going to be pulled, it is already sore from earlier treatment, so he'll stop. Believe me it does work but the farmers don't like it as it is at a slower pace.

At the time there were in the South of France oxen educated in all sorts of Dutch songs, rude and otherwise, and a farmhand with a very sore throat.

Another job I liked was herding, once a day after work, the two oxen and the milk cow, and letting them graze on the sparse dry vegetation. I had thereby the assistance of the two farm dogs. My favourite was Marquise; she loved me – probably because I never kicked her. These dogs were unbelievably alert. The kine, as soon as they were released to graze, made for the unfenced rows of grapevines. As soon as those two dogs saw them making towards the vines they were off chasing them back to their grazing. They must have been mind-readers. As soon as the job was done back they came to lie at my feet wagging their tails.

Yet another job was mucking out the stable and the pig sties. When the oxen and the horse were at work the cow was temporarily put in another place for the work to be done. There was the only small fenced-off bit in the yard where the chickens were kept; otherwise it would have been too time-consuming to find and collect the eggs. There was a sty for the pigs which was also used by the farmhand as a lavatory after first collecting a leaf from the lavatera shrub.

Apart from the buildings described, there was a large cellar housing the vast fermenting and storage vats. The open fermenting vats were about five foot high and large enough to set out a three piece suite of furniture. They were towards the grape harvest splashed daily with water to swell the staves and make them watertight – extra work for the water carrier. The same happened to the large enclosed vats after they had been scraped of the wine tartar, a precious commodity, and fumigated with sulphur candles.

The working day ran from before sunrise to after sundown, which in summer is a long time. The first job at daylight and before breakfast was pulling up a row or two of beans. The plants were very dry and could only be pulled out when the ground was still damp with dew. This was very sore on the hands and back from bending. The plants were threshed on a spread tarpaulin to get the beans out. The haulms[7] were used for bedding for the animals.

Then after breakfast of bean soup with pieces of bacon and porridge with home-baked bread washed down with black "coffee", I was given my first task for the day or taught those tasks I was not familiar with.

While I worked on the farm the time for the "dépicage" (threshing) came, and one fine day a steam-driven road tractor towing a threshing machine arrived on the farm, to start operating the next day. Early in the morning men and women from surrounding farms turned up to help; the men with the threshing and the women to help the farmer's wife with the preparation of the food to feed the men. When the last sheaf had gone through the machine, the straw was built into a new stack and the chaff was stored to serve as winterfeed for the animals.

For the meal a long table was set out in the open covered with white sheets; forms made of planks resting on crates set around it. For the soup spoons were provided; no doubt brought along by the women. But for the rest of the meal there was no cutlery. Everyone took out their clasp knife to convey the food from the large platters to the mouth. So did Frans, who was also at the party, and I using our camping knives. Living dangerously!

One of the dishes stands firmly engraved in my mind: fried goat nuggets with garlic. The smell of garlic was all prevailing and there were huge bowls filled with these bulbs on the table for everyone (except two) to eat of them as if they were sweets. The next day the itinerant threshing cavalcade moved off to the next farm, and the day after all was repeated

---

7 The stems or tops of crop plants (such as peas or potatoes) especially after the crop has been gathered.

and we turned up for another day's work and feasting. Unnecessary to record the quantities of wine consumed at these do's - to my estimation enough to sink a battleship, or at least a frigate.

Not so long after came the time for the "vendange" (grape harvest and wine making). Here Frans and I met again at my farm and were given the job of carrying the large bucket-like container, strapped to our back, along the line of grape pickers for them to empty their baskets into. Then we took it to the end of the row, there to empty it in the vats on cart or wagon. When full the cart or wagon would take the grapes to the wine cellar to be crushed, and via a chute into the enormous fermentation vats. It took a few days to harvest all the grapes on the farm. The must in the huge vats was kept down by means of a large oaken trellis kept submerged with poles jammed against the ceiling. After the must had been fermenting for some time the partly fermented liquid was drawn off through a filter of twigs, and pumped into the large storage vats to continue the fermentation process.

In the mean time a large press had arrived at the farm into which the pulp, consisting of the skins, pips, leaves and stalks, was shovelled and when full the press was turned, squeezing out the juice until nothing more came out. This juice was the farmers perk as the wine had already been sold whilst on the vine to a wine merchant. Some of this juice went to the local distillery to be turned into "Eau de Vie" (water of life). Some water!

After the press was dismantled the now solid cake of skins, pips and stalks was shovelled out onto the yard to serve as food for the cattle. The press was taken away to the next farm with a vineyard.

Soon there was a visit from the wine merchant to test the wine and estimate the number of barrels required to transport the wine to the blending house. After the barrels arrived they were laid in long rows with bungholes uppermost. They too had to be fumigated first with sulphur candles hung from wire in the barrels; then they were partly filled with water and rolled so that all the staves became swollen and the barrels watertight. Now could begin the task of filling the barrels with the fermented wine. Each filled barrel was bunged and after the last one was filled the rolling could begin. One empty barrel was positioned at the end of each line and filled from its neighbour, and so on in turn until there was an empty one on the other end. This process was repeated time and again to stop further fermentation.

It now came to pass that the swine had to be mucked out. The usual *procedure was to turn them loose into the yard; clear out the old and put in the fresh bedding and entice them with some titbit back into their home. This time however they had found the pile of grape pulp and were greedily feeding from it. There was no way to get them away from this delicious alcoholic repast. They were already drunk as lords and were not to be persuaded to go home. It was a hilarious job with all hands to get them one by one, squealing and falling over drunkenly, back to their abodes, there to sleep it off.*

Another feast was when the butcher came to the farm to slaughter one of the fattened pigs to make it into provisions for the winter. The carcase was cut into flitches for dry-curing in salt, then to be hung in the chimney to be smoked over the wood burning cooking fire. There was the meat for making into sausages and the offal. Again women from nearby farms came to help with all the preparations. That evening we feasted on the offal and the delicious spiced sausages; all washed down with oodles of red wine.

Chapter 8

In and Around Fals

Piet's account of life on a French farm in the 1940s makes fascinating reading, as it evokes a distant and alien lifestyle. When we reached the Standaerts' farm after being directed from Fals, we found an almost idyllic and peaceful landscape, with smart farm buildings set among carefully tended fields – an almost complete contrast to the picture in our minds from reading Piet's book. At the entrance to the farm track was a wooden sign labelled 'Sabathe', the actual name of the farm. We drove down the track and parked in the farmyard, and were greeted by a somewhat puzzled farmer, surprised at this unexpected invasion by '*les Anglais*'.

The sign to the farm

The two farms at Sabathe

The main farmhouse

We explained our mission, and he announced that he was Bernard Standaert, grandson of the farmer that Piet worked for. He became friendlier, and told us that one of his cousins, another grandson, lived nearby in the larger village of Astaffort. We drove to Astaffort, found Cousin Marcel, and chatted to him. Neither he nor Bernard had any knowledge of Dutchmen working on the farm, which would have been before they were born.

Back in Agen, we visited the Departmental Archives of Lot-et-Garonne, and there had to register and get another set of reader's cards. A helpful and enthusiastic member of staff began dredging through the archives for information about the Standaerts and their farm. Eventually she found a record of the purchase of the farm in 1943 by Séraphin Standaert, so obviously his ownership was very new when Piet and Frans turned up. She also found a map of the property from 1836, which showed that it was not in the district of Fals but in Astaffort, even though Fals was the nearest village. This also confirmed the name of the farm: Sabathe.

The Standaert family

Knowing that the farmer was a resident of Astaffort explained why we had not found any family graves in the churchyard at Fals. However, in the cemetery at Astaffort we found two sets of family graves which helped to clarify the names and relationships of the Standaerts.

We found:
Séraphin Standaert: 22/7/1880 to 31/1/1963
Maria Standaert (née de Zutter):   2/7/1886 to 22/5/1972
Aimé Standaert: 13/6/1920 to 16/10/2005
Madeleine Standaert (née Van den Bon):   25/10/1927 to 10/11/2003
René Standaert: 3/3/1912 to 9/11/1980
Marie Standaert (née Van den Bon):   20/8/1920 to 14/12/2006

Standaert gravestone

Ian and Bernard Standaert

Sandie with Marcel Standaert

Clearly Séraphin was the original farmer who bought Sabathe, presumably having moved to the South of France from his native Belgium, and Maria was his wife. They would have been 63 and 57 in 1943, when Piet met them – no wonder he calls Maria *'a prematurely old woman'*. René would have been the elder son, married to Marie, and owner of the adjacent farm where Frans worked. They would have been 31 and 23 in 1943, and already married. Aimé would have been the younger son, who slept in the store room with Piet – he would have been 23. His wife Madeleine must have been sister or cousin to Marie, and would have been just 16 then. Presumably they married after the war.

We believe Bernard, who currently runs Sabathe, is the son of René, while Marcel is the son of Aimé.

Completing formalities

One fine day two gendarmes on their round came to the farm and spotted me. They wanted to know if I was family, or who. When told that I was a foreign worker M. Standaert was advised that I, and also Frans, should be brought to the Gendarmerie in Astaffort to have our papers seen to. This we had dreaded all the time we were on the loose in France and now it had come. We had so hoped to receive a call from Mr Aarts before this should happen; but now there was no getting out of it. The next day, old man Standaert in his Sunday suit, Frans and I went on three excuses for bicycles – without brakes – down the hill to the small town of Astaffort and its Gendarmerie.

There, Frans and I were led into an office whilst my "patron" had to stay in the guardroom. Behind the desk in the office sat a very obese sergeant, who began by asking all the usual questions: name, date of birth, where born, nationality, etc. etc. "So we were Hollandais?" As by magic his attitude changed and he became less stern and more affable. He now told us that he had been to Holland, in 1940, when his regiment had been rushed there to help the Dutch Forces stem the German invasion; but had to return to France before being overrun. He had been in the area around Breda and had been very well received and treated by the Dutch people, who were not like "les boches"!

He then began to explain that he would have to make a "process verbal" (take down our statement in writing) upon which he could apply on our behalf for the papers to make our stay in the "arrondissement" (district) "en règle" (legal). All we had to do was to sign the statement after it was typed and get two passport photos to him. And as soon as these were in his possession it was only a matter of a few days and we could collect from his office our residence permits. Our patron was called into the office and told that he would not be in trouble as he had brought us to him "voluntarily" and to get our pictures to him soonest.

We parted from our friend the sergeant with hand-shakes to the surprise of my overawed employer. In a much relieved mood at the unexpected outcome we cycled back up the hill, counting ourselves lucky that this happened so far away from Vatan.

The morning after our visit to our genial policeman we, my boss, again in his Sunday best, Frans and I, mounted the bikes and went to the provincial town of Agen to have "our portraits taken". In Agen lived a man, Monsieur Jaminet, who regularly visited the farm to do "business", the character of which it was better not to enquire into; but he left with his bicycle laden with produce such as almonds, dried prunes, eggs, butter and such like.

After our pictures were taken – paid for by my patron, to be collected later – we paid a visit to M Jaminet, a very congenial fellow, who took the two of us to the market while my boss conducted some business of his own. With our portraits safely in M. Standaert's wallet we rode back into the hills and home.

Frans and I went alone the next day to the Gendarmerie to hand in our pictures and were told to call back in two days to collect and sign our passes. We still weren't sure whether we were taken for a ride as it all seemed too good to be true. Two days later we were received as old friends, signed some documents and received our passes; were told "Maintenant vous êtes en règle" but must not move out of the district without prior permission.

Very much relieved at the outcome we returned "home" to our respective farms and told them there that all was sorted out and that we were now legally there showing our "récipissée's" (authority to reside), but forgot to tell them about the notice [not to leave the district].

This seems a good point at which to express our gratitude to all those people in France, and elsewhere, who so unstintingly, and at enormous risk to themselves, helped us on our passage through their country.

We found the *gendarmerie* in Astaffort, though it is quite new and may not be in the same location as in the 1940s. We were unable to track down the photographer's shop in Agen, or M Jaminet, though we did visit the market near the Garonne, which may have been the same one Piet mentions.

Time off work

Once per week we had our four hours of liberty, on either Saturday afternoon or Sunday morning. On the Saturday we went to Astaffort on the bike to look at the shops or have a haircut; then on our way back we stopped off at a lonely spot on the river Gers to have our weekly bath, shave and shampoo in the river and do our laundry. Bathing trunks were unnecessary as there was never anybody about. After that we returned home with our handlebars festooned with wet underwear.

On Sunday mornings we went to [a] different bathing place on the same river where there was a weir by a disused mill. The water was much deeper and clearer and better for swimming. We picked ripe figs from a tree overhanging the river, and almonds and prunes from a deserted orchard. The prunes we used to lay in the sun to dry and to be collected on a later visit. Four hours in the life of Riley! with not a soul in sight.

By 'prunes' he doubtless means plums. To get a feel for these weekend jaunts we decided to walk the road from Fals to Astaffort and back. Passing Sabathe farm we noted a second entrance track, also signed 'Sabathe' which led to another building somewhat separate from the one we had visited. This was doubtless the satellite farm run by the elder son, where Frans worked.

On the way down into Astaffort the road passes close to a bend in the river Gers, and we detoured to walk along the bank. We found a secluded spot which must have been the one Piet mentions, or close to it. The river certainly did not look too inviting for swimming – it was light brown in colour, like thin mud.

We were also looking for the place near the disused mill where they went on Sundays. In Astaffort there is an old mill where the main road crosses the river, but it is anything but secluded and is unlikely to be the place Piet describes. Walking back up to Fals, we passed a sign saying 'Moulin de Roques', and followed that track until we reached a mill and

The swimming place by the road

weir at a very quiet spot by the river. The mill had been renovated and was inhabited, but in 1943 may have been deserted. There was no-one around, so we explored the river bank, which seemed to be much as Piet describes. We could not identify all the fruit trees he speaks of, though they may have been removed or died in the last 72 years.

After all our researches we now felt that we had a good understanding of the

The swimming place at the old mill

area where Piet and Frans spent the two months of their rural 'idyll' – but now it was time to move on to the Pyrenees.

Chapter 9

Over the Pyrenees

Piet and Frans were keen to continue their journey to Spain, and were frustrated at having to wait. So they decided to take matters into their own hands.

One day I wrote to M. Aarts asking him when we could expect to be called for crossing the mountains to Spain as autumn was approaching and soon the passage would be impossible. We could see already the snow-capped peaks in the distance. No reply was received, so we made up our minds to abscond to Toulouse on Monday 20 September and thus present Mr. Aarts with a "fait accompli". Our next free time was on Sunday 19 September; we had our usual swim at the weir, did our washing and planned our getaway for early the next morning.

Monday 20 September was the 91st day after leaving Zaandam, and very early in the dark, while the family Standaert was sound asleep – including my room-mate the son – I sneaked out in my stockinged feet. My rucksack was waiting in the stable, where I had hidden it the day before, and hanging it on I proceeded to our agreed rendez-vous. It was half past four and in the pitch black we marched to Agen, some eight miles away. We had arranged to meet M. Jaminet at his home, where he gave us breakfast and saw us off at the railway station. The rail fare took almost all our money as we had left without our back pay. We did not want the Standaerts to know we were going in case they got cold feet and informed on us to the gendarmes.

When we arrived at M. Aarts's office he seemed not to be perturbed at our appearing there, and arranged for accommodation with another widow, Madame Passaret, in the Rue Beau Site, whose bungalow bordered at the rear on the airfield where we noticed a great many German military aircraft. We had to find the bungalow without the help of Joop van Dam who had already left across the Pyrenees. M Aarts had told us that we would shortly be leaving for Spain, as he was expecting the arrival of a party of escapers from Switzerland.

Piet and Frans did what the Scots would call 'a moonlight flit', due possibly to paranoia or perhaps a realistic concern about Séraphin Standaert's reaction to their leaving. As it happened, they returned to Toulouse without incident, there to await their journey over the Pyrenees.

It is interesting that a party of escapers from Switzerland would be joining them, in the light of Piet's debate about their route when they first reached France. Switzerland was neutral, but very much a 'dead end', as to reach Allied territory you would need to pass through Axis-controlled lands. Spain was obviously a better option – if you could get there.

A surprise encounter

In Toulouse we decided to search for the home of Mme Passaret in the Rue Beau Site. It is a fairly short road, with only two bungalows. It was impossible to tell which was the right one. We began to examine the name plates on the gates, when a woman came up and asked us (reasonably) what we were doing – the local equivalent of Neighbourhood Watch. When we explained our quest, she told us that there was an old lady at number 4 who had lived there all her life and might be able to help. We knocked at the two-storey house, and asked the lady who answered if she could tell us where Mme Passaret used to live. She said *'She used to live here – she was my mother!'* We were astonished, and burbled something about her living in a bungalow. The lady smiled and said they had added an extra floor since 1943!

She invited us inside, and we had a pleasant time chatting to her and her husband – their surname now was Odinot. They gave us a drink, and showed us the view downhill from the back, which now looked over a new housing estate rather than a German airfield. Mme Odinot said she had been a little girl in the war, but did not remember Dutchmen staying

M and Mme Odinot

in the house, as she had been sent to stay with relatives in the mountains. One of her cousins was a 'passeur', who helped escapers to cross the Pyrenees. Presumably that explained the link between Mme Passaret and M Aarts. They showed us photos of Mme Passaret and the house when it used to be a bungalow.

No. 4 Rue Beau Site, as a bungalow

We left number 4 Rue Beau Site, amazed and delighted that, by pure serendipity, we had managed to meet another relative of someone who had helped Piet and Frans!

We stayed with Mme Passaret from 20 to 28 September and, as at this time there were no restrictions on our movements, we felt reasonably at ease in the town. The Germans had by now occupied Vichy France and whenever we felt conspicuous we dived into a newsreel cinema to be regaled by German victories. I also watched a German feature film "Die Goldene Stadt" with subtitles in French, but cannot remember the story.

Mme Passaret and daughter

'Die Goldene Stadt' is a 1941 German film. Anna, a young, innocent country girl, whose mother drowned in a swamp, dreams of the golden city of Prague. After she falls in love with a surveyor, she runs away to Prague to find him. She is instead seduced and abandoned by her cousin (a Czech). She attempts to return home, but her father rejects her, and she drowns herself in the swamp where her mother died. It does sound fairly forgettable.

M. Aarts had provided us with a little pocket money. We met in Toulouse another Dutch escaper, Hut by name, who asked us if we could help him out as he had lost his money. How was not quite clear. We regretted that we could not help him as we had very little money between us.

Preparing for departure

Sunday 26 September; we received at Mme Passaret a message for one of us to call at M. Aarts's office the next day to attend a pre-departure briefing and receive our instructions. Frans agreed that I should go, and at

*the office I met for the first time three of our travelling companions: Gazan,
Beets and later Hans Mol.*

*We had to restrict our luggage to the absolute minimum – the rest
could be left behind at the office to be picked up after the war (!) – and
to dress as warmly as possible. The meeting place would be at the bridge
over the canal in front of the main station at eight sharp the next morning.
There we would be given by a lady our train tickets. We had to follow the
lady, who would be carrying a shiny black shopping bag, two by two, at
distances of a hundred paces. We were not to speak to her nor to show any
sign of recognition. She would board a train in one of the front carriages
and we had to follow her on to the train, again two by two, but in different
compartments. When she left the train we had to do the same, still keeping
our distances.*

*The last part of the journey would be on foot and the separation had
to be maintained. It seemed well organised, and back at our lodgings I
gave Frans a résumé of what had transpired at the meeting. We began
immediately to sort out what of our possessions to take with us and what
to leave behind at the office. As it was an unknown factor how long the
war would last we didn't expect to see any of what went to the office ever
again. What was to come with us was to be packed in Frans' rucksack
as this was the lightest and had an aluminium frame, which made it
more comfortable to carry than mine which was larger and heavier.
We also expected to have to cross some heavy terrain and possibly meet
some snow-covered ground as well. Sturdy footwear was a prerequisite
and we had those, woollen socks, puttees to bridge the gap and our plus
four trouser bottoms. Over our underwear we would wear our flannel
pyjama bottoms, woollen shirt, woollen sweater; then our pyjama tops
and our waterproof jackets. Frans had a wind- and water-proof anorak
and I a warm waterproof lumber jacket. For head cover we both had our
Basque berets. I also took my military cape. In the rucksack we stowed
an extra set of underwear, spare socks, the little spirit cooker with metal
bottle of spirits, toilet things and razors, soap, towels and a tie each – for
special occasions !*

*All the rest including our instruments were packed in or with my
rucksack and in the afternoon deposited in a cupboard at the office.*

After a long period of fending for themselves and travelling randomly,
Piet and Frans were now clearly in the hands of a highly organised, if

clandestine, setup. It would be interesting to know what happened to the goods they left behind in M Aarts's office.

The group sets off

The big moment arrived, Tuesday 28 September, when our complete party assembled for the first time at the canal bridge opposite the station. Our 'passeuse' arrived at half past eight: a woman of indeterminate age and nondescript appearance, but carrying a large shiny bag which flashed in the sunlight. She handed each of us our ticket in silence and moved off into the station. Our party of seven followed her as per our instructions. First Nico Gazan and Jan Hoezen, followed by Beets and Lathouwers, then Hans Mol on his own and Frans and I as the last pair; all at 100 paces distance. Inside the station the lady must have boarded a train and so did each couple in turn until we were all aboard.

The train left at 8:40 and was one of the slow local variety. Whenever the train halted heads would pop out of compartment windows to see if she alighted. At 11:25 we reached Montréjeau where we left the train to board another waiting across the platform. It was the 11.30 to Bagnieres-de-Luchon, a well-known spa in the Pyrenees. Some little time later we got off at Loures-Barbazan, and following our guide in the same formation we marched in procession south in the direction of the Franco-Spanish border.

On the way Hoezen, Beets and Mol were stopped by a gendarme, but Frans and I had spotted the danger [and] had dived behind a low wall until the danger was over, when the gendarme cycled past our hiding place. We continued marching until the small railway station of Saléchan, where the stationmaster welcomed us and led us to his home above the station. We learned that the policeman was a "good one" because when he was told that they were on their way to Spain he let them pass with a "Bon voyage".

We bade farewell to our 'passeuse', and after darkness had fallen were led, again in twos – and one – by the stationmaster's very young daughter to the hotel "Lamolle" in Siradan. She seemed very experienced at it and must have done that job before. In the hotel were rooms and a meal for our party, and we were acquainted with all our companions. They had come via Switzerland along an organised escape route. They were all dressed

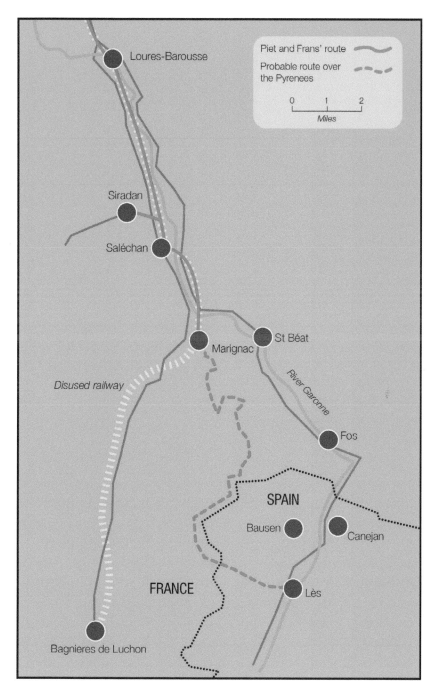

Legend:
Piet and Frans' route
Probable route over the Pyrenees

0   1   2
Miles

Loures-Barousse

Siradan

Saléchan

Marignac

St Béat

River Garonne

Disused railway

Fos

SPAIN

Bausen

Canejan

FRANCE

Lès

Bagnieres de Luchon

Crossing the Pyrenees

in city suits with gabardine raincoats and trilby hats, low shoes and thin socks. Quite a collection of businessmen on an outing.

Returning to Toulouse from Agen, we went outside the station to find the canal bridge where the escapers waited, and then back inside to catch the train down to Montréjeau. The line south from Montréjeau to Bagnières-de-Luchon had been closed, and there was now a bus service to take us onward.

We had struggled to find accommodation for our stay in the French Pyrenees, and in the end had booked into a *chambre d'hôte* in Marignac, a little village on the old line south of Montréjeau, close to the mountains. We caught the bus and got off at the old station at Marignac, before facing a long uphill climb with our case to the accommodation. We were made very welcome by our hosts there, and spent five nights in total perched on the mountainside, with panoramic views over the Garonne valley.

The following day we took the bus back north to the village of Loures-Barosse, where the old station for Loures-Barbazon is situated (confusingly, the town of Loures-Barbazon is further away, on the other side of the river). The station had been converted into offices, but we walked into the village to get coffee and buy some walking maps of the local mountains. We returned to the station and began walking south, following the escapers' route, on a track which mostly followed the disused railway line but at one point went alongside the Garonne.

Eventually we reached the station at Saléchan, now converted into a smart house. We had a snack lunch on the old platform, and then struck away from the road and railway towards the village of Siradan, a little way to the west. We imagined the Saléchan stationmaster's young daughter leading her little party along the country roads. It seems that people in the Resistance made good use of young girls to divert suspicion from their activities.

In Siradan we initially struggled to find any trace of the Hotel Lamolle, and wandered through the village looking for any sign of life. We found a couple in their garden and asked for help, and they were able to give us directions to a large building opposite the Mairie, now no longer a hotel but converted into a private house. We visualised the party of escapers waiting there, hidden from sight, Piet and Frans kitted out for the mountains and the Swiss contingent in their smart suits.

Saléchan station

Hotel Lamolle in Siradan

We were to remain in our rooms for the whole of 29 September, except for meals. After dinner a guide arrived, and sometime later a second one, to meet us and give advice and instructions about what was to come. We had an Armagnac on the successful outcome. One of the guides stayed with us at the hotel whereas the other one, for whom the ground was too hot, disappeared. We had been advised to go early to bed as we would be making a start at 4:30 the next morning.

After the war I learned that Mr. Aarts died in front of a German firing squad.

A poignant comment – but we have been unable to find any information about M Aarts.

In the pitch dark the next morning, the last day of September 1943, we set off in our socks so as to make no noise on the roads in the village. It had been rumoured that there had been a German patrol through the village during the night. The guide who had stayed with us at the hotel was leading the party through the sleeping village until once outside we could put on our footwear again as we now moved through the open country looking for gaps in fences, skirting large puddles as it had been raining during the night. This had been the first rain during all our time in France. We reached the main road again, which we crossed in line abreast. After that we reached the railway line which we followed, ever going south, sometimes walking on the sleepers between the rails or on either side of the single track.

We marched in the same formation as when we left Toulouse. After about an hour of this we met the other guide, whom we took to be the chief. He produced from a sack three revolvers which he gave to those who had used firearms before: Gazan, Hoezen and me[8]. The six-shooter I was entrusted with was so rusty that I would be scared to use it if it came to that. We were put at ease however as they were not to shoot at German patrols or guards, as we were assured by our guides that the Germans avoided the convoys of crossers in the "zone interdite" as they knew these were armed. No, they were against the bears who still roamed these mountains in the wild. And even they were more interested in the sheep and goats. Fortunately we did not encounter either Germans or bears.

Having climbed steadily through the wooded slopes we were now

---

8   Piet was 'armed with a pistol' when working as a customs officer. See Appendix A.

above the treeline, and out of the shelter of the pinewoods it became much windier and colder. The low shrubs that now covered the mountain slopes gave less shelter. Coming from a country renowned for its flatness and low lying terrain we now became aware of the wildness of these mountains. All romantic notions disappeared and we wondered what we had let ourselves in for.

From Siradan we walked back to the main road and the railway line and headed south as they did. However, now Piet's account becomes much less explicit about the route they followed, so all we could do was to head south back to Marignac and then find a suitable route over the mountains. We reached a point where we had to cross the Garonne, and ended up walking across on the railway tracks – just as Piet and his companions did. When we reached Marignac we looked for a café, and in the end were given drinks by a group of locals playing *boules* in the village square. We climbed back up to our accommodation and prepared ourselves to tackle the mountains tomorrow.

The path to the Pyrenees

Along the tracks

Climbing the mountains

Of our group Frans and I were the best equipped and prepared for the rigours to come. The other five having come from the civilisation of Switzerland and in their business suits and little suitcases were hardly dressed for the rugged terrain. Neither did any of them carry with them any provender to sustain them. Frans and I had with us the means of heating water and food and a store of bacon, tea, bread and lump sugar for energy, "borrowed" from the farm in lieu of wages. Also, through our labours on the way south we were physically in a fit condition without an ounce of surplus weight. Before leaving home I had been reading some books about mountains.

That shows a great deal of forward planning, though probably the books had not prepared him fully for the reality!

At about four in the afternoon, after stumbling over the rock-strewn mountain slopes, we reached the snowline where we made a halt in a snow-free hollow, sheltered from the icy wind. Here the two 'passeurs' showed us the way to continue to reach Spain. We were still in France! They collected their shooters and returned in the direction from which we had come.

One of our party, at 35 years the eldest, had been exhausted for some time and the six of us had carried him one at each side whilst a third carried his pathetic little suitcase. This we had to do in relays in the rarefied atmosphere high in the mountains. It was therefore decided not to continue, and to stop in the hollow to give our sick companion the rest he so badly needed.

This decision was however not unanimous. Lathouwers did not agree and wanted to go on. We had had our doubts about Lathouwers' nationality since he spoke no Dutch but Flemish and Walloon French. Challenged he produced from a tooth-paste tube, a rolled up Netherlands passport without its cover wrapped in a rubber sheath in the name of Lathouwers and bearing his photograph. It had been issued to him by the Dutch Consul in Switzerland, so he said. He set off on his own, leaving the remaining five of us with our sick friend. We met later with him again.

During the bitter cold night in our hollow, there high up in the unfamiliar mountains we huddled together for warmth and sharing little pieces of salty bacon to chew and sugar lumps to suck for energy. Snow was thawed on our little spirit flame. It takes a lot of snow to produce a very little water to wet the lips. Frans and I had the extra shelter of my cloak which buttoned up made into a little tent. But the others had only their thin raincoats.

Piet does not say which of his companions fell sick – possibly to save him embarrassment. However, he later refers to Nico Gazan, 'who had such an awful time in the mountains' (Chapter 11) and mentions Nico's 'exhaustion on the climb through the mountains' (Chapter 13). It seems likely that he was referring to this incident.

For our part we set off from Marignac to see how high we could get into the mountains, and whether we could find a path that would take us towards Spain. As we were over twice the age that Piet was when he made his crossing we did not expect to get right to the top, but wanted to explore the French side of the Pyrenees as much as we could. At Marignac we found a monument to those who crossed the Pyrenees in the war and those who helped them. From there we climbed up steadily, following well-marked paths through the trees, but never getting above the forest.

In the mountains

On our map we found a path marked that zigzagged up and seemed to head towards the border, so we decided to give it a go. We had lunch at a mountain hut at the foot of the path and headed up. Soon we reached the zigzags, and then our problems began. The way became very steep and overgrown, and the exact path difficult to discern. We struggled on up, but in the end had to confess ourselves beaten, even though we were still below the tree line. We returned to Marignac by a different route, passing another mountain hut where a kind soul had left a couple of bottles of wine to refresh weary hikers. We took some sips to fortify us for the way back.

We woke up to the most glorious sunrise. The glow of the sun rising in the east painted the snow-covered tops a brilliant rosy pink. But it lasted not long. We had to go on. There was no sign of "Lathouwers". What the opinion of the others was on the matter of his leaving, Frans and I did not know at the time, but we were disgusted with such behaviour. There is a Dutch saying: "Out together, Home together".

Those who had taken off their shoes during the night to relieve their aching feet now regretted that deeply, as these were now frozen solid and had to be thawed first before they could be put on.

After setting off again, supporting our comrade, we traversed a saddle and along a comb with precipitous slopes on both sides before we saw far down below a little clump of houses by a road and river in the valley. Not knowing where we were we hoped nevertheless that it was the "Val d'Aran", the course of the river Garonne on the Spanish side with the village of Lès.

Interestingly, though we were in the Pyrenees at about the same time of year as Piet, we saw no sign of snow on the peaks which form the border between France and Spain. Perhaps the difference is due to global warming over the past 72 years.

The following day we took a break from our pursuit of Piet and Frans, and took the bus to Bagnières-de-Luchon, where we spent some pleasant hours exploring the little spa town. The day after, however, we determined to reach the Spanish border, even if we had to do it along the road. We left Marignac again but this time walked on the road which heads southeast to the Spanish border, following the course of the Garonne. We passed through the very attractive village of St Béat and carried on to Fos, close to the border. The road had a lot of traffic on it, mainly heavy lorries crossing from France to Spain or vice versa, through one of the few passes which allow passage between these countries across the Pyrenees.

St Béat on the Garonne

Finally we reached the border, marked by a blue EU flag with 'España' in the centre. There were also signs welcoming us to the Val d'Aran, and a poster giving some of the history of the escapers from Nazi tyranny, mainly Jews, who crossed to Spain there. The poster also featured photos of stern-looking border guards, though when we came there we found no sign of any border security, apart from an abandoned customs post a few miles back. We had arrived in Spain, the first country Piet reached which was not directly controlled by the Nazis.

Spain at last!

We went back to Marignac and then returned to Toulouse, to fly home for a wedding and family business. We were to pick up the trail again from the Spanish side of the mountains.

Border guards during WW2

Chapter 10

Arrival in Spain

More than three months after leaving the Netherlands, Piet and Frans finally found themselves in Spain.

Our descent was even more exhausting than the ascent had been the previous day. There were no paths we could find, but [we] used, wherever we could, the rocky bottoms of dried up mountain streams, considering ourselves lucky that the snow was not melting. Frequently we had to make the descent on the seat of our pants. I had sewn the leather seat from my army riding breaches on to my plus fours, not knowing how these would stand up, and so preserved my decency.

In the late afternoon of the 1st of October we arrived in the valley, which indeed was that of the Garonne in Spain and at the little place called Lès. Our welcoming party consisted of one man in civilian clothes with a peaked army cap and carrying on his shoulder a rifle on a piece of string. He led us to the local lock-up where we were searched and all sharp objects taken from us, including the safety-pins from my "housewife". We then had to write our names in a book and were escorted to the local hotel "Franco-Espagnol", where we had our first real meal since the morning the day before in Siradan, and another one at ten, the usual time in Spain for dinner. One of our party had been in touch by telephone with our Consulate in Barcelona who promised to foot the bill.

To reach the Spanish side of the Pyrenees we flew from England to Zaragoza, a city which we had visited before and thoroughly enjoyed. We hired a car at the airport and drove into the city centre for a one-night stay. We had drinks in the main square in front of the impressive Basilica del Pilar. In this and many other ways our travels were much easier than Piet's!

The following day (23rd September) we left Zaragoza and drove north towards the Pyrenees, via Huesca, with a stop in the picturesque hilltop town of Bennabarre. Then the road became more exciting: winding and narrow, with views of gorges, lakes and mountains. To reach the Val d'Aran there is a new 5-kilometre tunnel which took us through to the main town, Vielha. From there it was a short drive up the valley to the little village of Lès, nestled on the banks of the rushing Garonne, now more of a mountain stream than the broad placid river we had encountered in Agen and Toulouse.

We checked into a hotel by the river and went out to explore the village, which did not take long. Near the church was a small library, and there we found a very helpful young man who was able to tell us about the location of the Franco-Espagnol Hotel, on the main road. He told us that it was the place where all the refugees who came over the mountains were accommodated, until onward transportation for them could be arranged. Over the years it had sheltered a large number of different people, though now it was closed. We were also able to obtain a map of walking trails in the mountains.

Hotel Franco-Espagnol

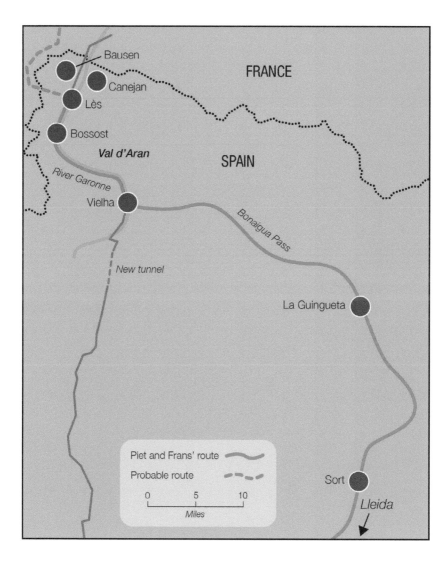

Val d'Aran, Sort and on to Lleida

The following day we set off, determined to explore some of the mountain regions even if we could not trace the exact route taken by Piet and his companions. We walked through Lès and began climbing steeply uphill, until we reached a crossing path which tracked around the mountainside. From there we had a clear view down to Lès lying in the valley below, as Piet saw it when he crossed the mountains. Heading north, eventually we reached the mountain village of Bausen, where we found a pleasant little bar to have our morning coffee.

Looking down on Lès

Lès and the Garonne

From Bausen there was a circular path winding further up the mountain, with views over to the French border. The path went through some woods, and then out on to open moorland with views on all sides. Only far off in the distance were there signs of snow on the very highest peaks. Looking round, we decided that Piet and his companions must have crossed further south, just to the west of Lès, where there were no paths marked, and they had to slide down on their bottoms. The path we were on went steeply downhill over open moorland, bringing us back to Bausen, where we had another drink before returning to Lès.

The following day we decided to walk to the border crossing with France, which we had reached two weeks earlier coming from the other direction. We set out along the road, soon passing the Hotel Franco-Espagnol, an old 3-storey building with the name still displayed on one end in large letters. The road was busy with heavy lorries thundering across the Pyrenees between France and Spain, and after a while we took a footpath which skirted the flanks of the mountains to the east. This eventually led us to another footpath sloping steeply uphill, to the village of Canejan on the side of the mountain overlooking the valley.

The detour seemed enticing, so off we went, zigzagging up and up until finally we reached the edge of the village, emerging near a small bar which offered us much-needed refreshment. Near the church was a sweeping view over the Val d'Aran and the surrounding mountains, with a glimpse of snowy peaks far off in the distance.

We returned from Canejan to the main road, and walked along in the face of the oncoming juggernauts, until we reached the Pont de Rei and the border, approaching from the Spanish side this time. After a few photos we turned round and walked back to Lès, finding on the way a small bar for a drink and a footpath over the fields that took us away from the main road. We spent our last night in Lès, ready to follow Piet and his companions deeper into Spain.

On to Vielha

We were also informed that we would be leaving the following morning at eleven o'clock to Bosost, the next place inland. This time was later advanced to 6 o'clock. When the bus arrived at six it was full and we had to wait for the next one at eleven. We stopped at Bosost to pick up and set off passengers, and we went on to Viella[9] (altitude 971 metres, population 600). There we were first shown the inside of the jail; but only to register our names in a book. This we had to do ourselves as the authorities could not cope with the spelling of our names. Our friends from Switzerland recognised, scribbled on the whitewashed walls, some of the names of those who had passed through before them. We were billeted in hotel "Serrano" in very comfortable rooms. In the village store, "La Casa de Tarragon", was available cigarettes and chocolate in abundance to those with the money to pay for these luxuries. A telegram, giving the news and the names of the new arrivals, was sent to our Consul in Barcelona, who agreed to pay our hotel bill and also informed us that the military age in Spain was between the ages of 18 and 35 and that we had to amend our date of birth accordingly to stay out of prison later on.

We did later find to our cost that this information was either wrong or misunderstood because of language difficulty. Our Consul was a Spaniard and had only his mother tongue and a little French.

Sunday 3 October: after a good rest and with a stout breakfast inside him our invalid had recovered appreciably from his ordeal in the mountains and expressed his gratitude for getting him through. Strolling in the village we met three Belgian and three Dutch mountain crossers; two youngsters called Charls and Faber and a third Kees Verhoeff, an alias, whose second trip across France and the mountains it was.

On Monday we contacted the Consulate again, who authorised the issue of pocket money and said that we would be moved on to Sort, our next stopping place. Our representative there would be Sěnor Tous, another Spaniard who only spoke Spanish. At eleven that morning another Dutchman, Slooves, came tottering into Viella, accompanied by an officer of the Guardia Civil. He was wounded and bleeding after a forty foot fall in the mountains; not an unusual occurrence, as that had happened to the very well-known Dutch author Jan de Hartog as well. We did not see him again that day as at half past one our transport arrived to take us at two o'clock. That was an antediluvian wooden coach with doors on both sides of the rows of benches and running boards along the side very much like the railway coaches of old. At the front on the roof was a seat for three passengers with feet dangling above the driver's cab.

Just before departure five more Dutchmen arrived in the village: Van

---

9   Piet spells the town 'Viella', but the modern spelling is 'Vielha'.

Balen, "Johnnie" Hart, Kragt, Dirks and "another". These had to be left behind as there was no more place in the bus, inside or out.

From Lès we drove south down the Val d'Aran, with a brief stop at Bosost, which is an attractive little town straddling the river Garonne. Here the river is narrow and rushes swiftly down the valley on its shallow bed, rippling and gurgling and seeming to be in a hurry to reach France. Further upstream we reached Vielha, the main town of the valley, and began to search for the places mentioned by Piet during his stay there.

Bosost

At the Tourist Information office the young lady told us that the Hotel Serrano had been rebuilt, and was now the Hotel Rui Nere, which could be seen just across the river opposite her office. She also told us where the 'Casa de Tarragona' was – at number 40 on the street that ran alongside the river. We found the place, though it was closed and had a sign saying '*Cerrajeria*' (locksmith).

Vielha is a pleasant little town, and we sat in the main square opposite the church for morning coffee. We also looked inside the church, and it was only later that we were informed that the church was used as the prison

The church (and prison) at Vielha

during the Franco regime. This is where Piet and his companions would have registered before being billeted nearby in Hotel Serrano. Piet calls Vielha a 'village' in his day, but acknowledges that nowadays it is definitely a town, and a significant tourist centre for that part of the Pyrenees.

Viella is now a thriving ski resort, frequently entertaining the Spanish Royal Family on holiday. The new road to Lérida now passes through a long tunnel thus bypassing the old narrow potholed track we took.

Together with seven Frenchmen and Spanish women with baskets, some containing fowls, others occupying the roof seats we set off steadily climbing to 2000 feet with on the one side a steep wall where the track had been carved out of the mountainside and on the other a precipitous depth into a valley with a stream at the bottom. At times the track crossed via rickety bridges to the other side scaring us out of our wits. It must have been hair-raising for those whose fate it was to be seated on the roof of the swaying and hardly sprung vehicle. But then they must have had full profit of the beautiful view and the fresh air.

Somewhere halfway was a place where two vehicles could pass; there

Casa de Tarragona, Vielha

we changed transports and this time it was Frans, Beets and Hans Mol who "volunteered" to take the top seats. The "new" bus moves and sways perturbingly to reach the col at 2000 metres above sea level, as a notice proclaims. Going down the other side of the highest point we reached Sort at seven in the evening.

Our escort, two policemen of the Guardia Civil (the ones with the funny hats which we likened to typewriters) make us sign again our names in the "visitors' book", this time in the Ayuntamiento (town hall). Having had our warning, Frans, at 20, gave his age as 17 and I, aged 27, thought I could pass for 35. Outside the town hall the new arrivals were greeted by a number of compatriots, who were anxious to see if there were any known faces among us. Already there were the brothers Theo and Marcel Wachtel, Alfred Frank, Louis van Coevorden and quite a number of others. In procession we went to the hotel "Pessano", where again an enormous meal was served at which we were told that the next day at five in the morning all of us, old- and newcomers, would be leaving for Lérida, the capital of the eponymous[10] province of Catalonia[11].

The road over the mountains to the east of Vielha is steep, but in better condition and not as hair-raising as in 1943. At the top is the pass of Bonaiqua, which is a ski area in winter and has impressive views of the surrounding peaks. We had now left the valley of the Garonne, which we had encountered so often on our travels, from Montauban onwards.

The Pass of Bonaiqua

---

10   We think he means 'autonomous'.
11   Lérida (now called Lleida) is not actually the capital of Catalonia.

Driving back down the other side of the pass, we reached the village of La Guingueta, where we stopped for lunch and went for a short walk round a nearby small lake. On the hillside there were a couple of hidden gun emplacements, put there by Franco when he decided to fortify the border with France in the 1940s.

Discovery in Sort

Eventually we reached Sort, a medium-sized town on the route from the Val d'Aran to Lleida. Apparently, during World War II Franco was keen to round up everyone who crossed the Pyrenees, and flooded the border area with troops and police to make sure they were all apprehended. Sort was a major staging post for funnelling refugees and escapers to the main prison at Lleida.

In Sort we found a helpful Tourist Information Office. Here we learned that the Hotel Pessano is actually called Pessets. It is not clear if this is a Catalan version of the same name (adopted with the increase of Catalan independence following the end of the Franco regime), or if Piet just remembered it wrongly. It is clearly the same place, because plaques in town confirmed that it was where refugees and escapers were

accommodated while in transit through Sort. It is now the Café Pessets; the hotel has moved to a new building on the edge of the town.

Café Pessets is an impressive pink building adorned with carvings of flying mermaids – definitely the most striking building in town. We had a drink there, and were told that the owner would be around in the evening. We promised to return later, so we could meet him. A short way further on is the old town jail, now converted to a

Pessets Hotel, Sort

The old prison in Sort

museum commemorating all the people who passed through Sort as refugees during the war.

Inside we found a book with the names of all the people who passed through the town, arranged alphabetically. Eagerly we searched for Piet's name, but found no sign of 'Schagen' in the book. Disappointed, we went inside the jail itself – a small room with bare stone walls and a vaulted ceiling. On the far wall was a sheet of Perspex on which the names were inscribed again, but this time in the order of arrival in Sort. We searched through the list of names and found some that Piet mentions – 'Wachtel', 'Frank' and so forth. Among them we found the name 'Sehoguen, Pieter' and went 'Aha!' Clearly the local person who transcribed Piet's name into the official register struggled with his handwriting, but there it was, however mangled. Going back to the book, it was easy to find the same name listed there. It gave us a funny feeling to see the first piece of written evidence that Piet had actually passed through.

A variant spelling of 'Schagen'

We took some photos of the *Ayuntamiento*, and then returned to Café Pessets for some tapas and red wine. Inside there were some old photos, including one of a large group of refugees having a meal inside the former hotel. We met the proprietor, descendent of the original owner, and he gave us a small book about the history of the hotel. Later we had a drink in

Flying mermaid of freedom   *Dinner for escapees at the Pessets Hotel*

the new Hotel Pessets, before returning to our own hotel slightly out of town.

> *Wakened at half past four we ate our breakfast "on the hoof" until the bus arrived in which all the escapers, of varied nationality, had to find a seat. A second bus had to be called in. This was a lucky circumstance as the headlights on "our" bus were non-functional; but luckily those on the second did work, so that that one could lead the way along the road, which was only a slight improvement on the tracks we had travelled on before. Thus we set off again in the dark and it was with relief that we greeted the first light of day. The convoy halted at Balaguèr, there at a neat and clean roadside café we had some refreshment before setting off on the last stretch to our destination about 30 miles away. The road became wider and the paving was in better condition, improving the comfort of the passengers. It was now the turn of Alfred Frank and myself to mount to the top seats, where both of us wrapped up in my cloak discussed the finer points of the Jewish religion[12].*

---

12   This journey is mentioned briefly in a letter from Alfred Frank – see Chapter 12.

The following day we too set off on the road to Lleida, again in more comfort and on improved roads. We had a stop at the village of Gerri de la Sal, where we did a circular walk along the river and explored an old monastery and a Roman bridge. At Balaguèr we found a roadside café (perhaps not the same one where Piet stopped) and also took refreshments, before continuing our journey into the city of Lleida.

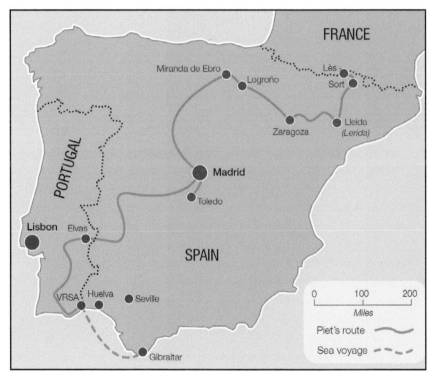

Piet's route through Spain and Portugal to Gibraltar

Chapter 11

A Prisoner in Spain

In October 1943, Piet and his companions arrived in Lleida:

> Our terminus in Lérida was at a small square in front of an ancient building, the Seminario Viejo (old Seminary). Whilst our transport left we were paraded in the square and those who had given their ages below 18, Frans, Hans Mol, Charls and Faber, were separated and the rest marched inside the building where we were greeted by some 170 internees already there.
>
> After the now customary registration we were first to have a haircut, right to the bone[13] (for hygienic reasons we were told), and issued with a "blanket", an aluminium bowl and a spoon. Mine had one side of the handle sharpened so that it could be used as a knife. Theo Wachtel obstinately refused to be scalped and was put in solitary confinement to consider the error of his ways and change his mind. We all had now changed from persons into "Lombroso type" individuals.

Piet's comment about 'Lombroso type' individuals is probably a reference to Cesare Lombroso (1835-1909), an Italian criminologist who claimed to be able to detect criminal types by physical features such as the shape of their skulls.

Lleida itself is a beautiful Catalan city, dominated by an old cathedral and castle perched on a hill. We arrived in the evening, checked into a

---

13   When Frans later visited Piet in prison, he wrote: '...they shaved him very bald. I could not recognize him.'

Lleida

hotel, and went to explore. Wandering the old city streets we came across a folk dance festival, which we enjoyed watching for a while. The lively music and dancing, and colourful costumes, formed a poignant contrast to the description of the internees' lives in Lleida in 1943.

Life in prison

Then to what were to be our quarters, upstairs in one of two open spaces with quarry tiled floors on which the marks of the cells of the former monks could be discerned. The only light to these spaces was through barred openings, without glazed windows, in opposite walls; one overlooking a blind wall and the other the courtyard, once the cloister. This served as exercise yard, for roll calls and where the food was cooked. There was no kitchen as such for the prisoners. The cooking arrangements were very simple: they consisted of two 2-foot high, parallel brick walls about two feet apart between which wood fires were lit. On these walls were placed the "cooking pots". These were the cut-off bottoms of 40 gallon drums, about 9 inches high and with wire handles.

Below the sleeping quarters at ground floor level was the earlier mentioned barbershop, the canteen and the open wash place. At certain times during the day water was available. This came from a horizontal galvanised pipe fixed to one wall. This pipe had no taps or faucets; instead it had at regular intervals holes drilled in it. These holes were closed with tapered pegs. To draw water, queues formed at each peg, one's bowl was held under and the peg removed and replaced for the next person to do the same until the water stopped coming. The water was for cleaning, washing (for those with soap) of clothes and self, if one had no open wounds or sores. For drinking and shaving it had first to be boiled. Those who drank the water regretted it later on. Over the sanitary arrangements it is better to draw a veil; also over the menagerie of vermin that shared our accommodation, and blood.

The food, such as it was, was once a day soup or thin stew in the pans or cauldrons described earlier. Whether stew or soup, water was boiled and into it went whatever was provided by the prison: onions quartered, chopped up root vegetables, cabbage, beans or peas, rice or maize (dried sweetcorn). As a speciality bones were sometimes added or bacon in the shape of pig's ears and other bits of their anatomy.

The Dutch contingent, which had increased to 29, was very lucky to get their food from the "chef". Señor Tous, our local Consular representative, had made arrangements with a local hotel, café or kitchen to have delivered to us a hot meal daily. This consisted invariably of a "one pan meal" like paella, or some suchlike appetising repast, together with a carboy of diluted wine (prison rule) and another with milk, a white roll and some fruit or other, banana, apple, peach or such, and was brought to the prison by a Spaniard with a donkey and cart. We took it in turns to bring it into the compound and act as mess boys. We were thus saved from starvation but it bore also other benefits because we never had to [clean] our bowls ourselves. For the privilege of cleaning our bowls, plus what we left in it, we had a personal "slave" who did that chore – and others – for us[14]. Any food left over in the cauldron was bartered for other commodities. The "washing

---

14 Piet does not explain who the 'personal slaves' were. We assume that they were non-Dutch prisoners.

up" was done by scouring our metal bowls with water and sand from the courtyard until they shone like mirrors.

With money comforts could be bought in the canteen. Things like sweets, chocolates, fruit, writing paper, envelopes and even postage stamps, razor blades, nuts and many other goodies. My first purchase was a sheet of paper, envelope and stamps, penholder with nib and a small bottle of ink to write to my family to let them know I was safe and so was Frans. The next was for a school exercise book. I was now equipped to draw up a calendar and itinerary since our travels began, noting dates, places, names and occurrences as these were still fresh in the memory. It served its purpose as an aide memoire in case it was needed later. And to good use it came.

The last section explains how Piet was able to write his detailed account of his travels in 1997, more than 50 years later, without needing to possess a supernatural memory. The exercise book clearly was put to good use.

We found already some Dutch "residents" at Lérida prison when we arrived: van der Weerd, "Meester" Fruin (an advocate): and also "Lathouwers", who had deserted us in the mountains. He never, to my knowledge, explained the reason for his conduct but admitted to being a Belgian national. After the war was over some investigation led me to a minor Belgian nobleman, the Chevalier André Lagasse de Locht in Antwerp. He maintained that he had received from a Dutch Consular official the passport of a Netherlands citizen, who at that time was still interned in Switzerland. I have never discovered how a consular official could issue to a foreign national a passport that had been surrendered to the consulate in case of unauthorised departure. Gazan, Hoezan, Mol and others told me they had to leave their passports at the consulate when they left Switzerland for France and Spain.

It is payday again on Wednesday 8 October[15]. We all, including "Lathouwers", receive another 50 pesetas pocket money. Also arrive van Balen, Dirks, Hart, Kragt and "Henco" Zwahlen. The strangest rumours are doing the rounds; one is of our incarceration here for months and months. Another is that of indeterminate detention in the concentration

---

15 Piet made a slight mistake with the date. It has to be 6 October, to fit with other dates given. This is confirmed by Frans's account, and by the Internet; 6 October, not 8 October, was a Wednesday in 1943.

camp of Miranda de Ebro. We are also to receive a visit from our consul in Barcelona and another from a chancellor at the embassy in Madrid; neither materialise.

Suddenly at seven in the evening we, the Dutch, are issued with a palliasse cover and a load of dry sweetcorn husks arrived in the courtyard. Hurriedly we started stuffing our covers and from that night on we do not have to search for a soft floor tile which fits our hipbone.

At the time of our incarceration we had daily visits from the "youngsters" who were at liberty outside and living it up in hotel rooms. Their number was increased by one, a newcomer Piet de Jong. They provided us with news from outside and cigarettes.

What kept the inmates awake at night were what the French called "punaises" (drawing pins). They were lice, which we called parachutists because of their habit of dropping from the ceiling onto the sleeping bodies below. During the day they hid in cracks and crevices in the wooden ceiling. At night they came out of their hiding places, crawled along the ceiling sensing for the rising warmth from a sleeper below. Then swollen with their victim's blood they climbed slowly aloft back to their hiding places.

That was why a "bug watch" was instituted. As it was not possible to prevent them from dropping, it was the task of the watch to prevent them reaching safety. Armed with a wad of toilet paper and a candle each watchman stood by his allocated piece of whitewashed wall to squash them one by one as they slowly climbed upwards. Each of us took his turn and very shortly the result was a bizarre mural painted in Allied blood. Another result of their bites were ulcers; Alfred Frank had to be treated in the sickbay.

It was said that there were means to ward them off, but the one was even more disgusting than the other. Fortunately I had brought with me from home, and had carried across the Pyrenees, a blue overall. Buttoned to the neck and tied around wrists and ankles with string, and with socks covering feet and hands I was almost bugproof with the exception of head and face. This I covered with a veil made from an Aertex vest. I never received a bite!

We spent a morning sightseeing in Lleida, including the impressive old cathedral and the castle. However, our chief aim was to identify the prison where Piet and his companions were interned. Our main clue was that he says it was an old seminary, and looking on the internet we found evidence that this could have been the former Bishop's Palace. On the other hand, at the Tourist Office they insisted that it was the building opposite, now part of the university.

We walked down to that part of the city and walked round both buildings, but were unable to determine which was used as a prison in 1943. Finally we rang the bell at the main door of the Bishop's Palace, now used as diocesan offices, and spoke to two members of staff. They told us clearly that the old seminary was not there, but was indeed the building over the road.

We crossed over and stood in the square in front of the imposing edifice, which now began to seem very prison-like, with towering stone walls and rows of narrow windows. There seemed to be no way of getting inside. We walked round to the back, where there was evidence of new construction, including a library, but everything was closed. This must have been the prison where Piet and the others were incarcerated, but it was as hard for us to get in as it was for them to get out.

Their prison in Lleida

Waiting to leave

Monday 11 October: no news yet of our departure and we wonder what is being done in Barcelona and Madrid to get us out of this place. Mr Fruin hears from the prison doctor that soon nine of us are being set free. In the afternoon we receive another 50 pesetas (20 pence in present day money) which is as much as a Spanish craftsman with a family earns in a week. Piet de Jong visits us and says that for each of us has arrived in the prison a suitcase containing two sets of underwear, socks, pull-over, soap and two tablets of chocolate. The same night the French receive each a white roll and half a packet of margarine which many promptly sell for 4 pesetas.

Amongst the new arrivals this day was one Dutchman who introduced himself as Linthorst Homan, a reputable name in Holland. He was one of the directors of Philips, the international electric company.

Tuesday 12 October. We were called to the prison office to have our fingerprints taken. That night we are plagued by the bugs and the bug watch report a "bag" of between seven and eight hundred killed in an area of ten square metres.

Thursday 14 October. Kragt is being taken into sick quarters suffering from a nasty infection.

The number of inmates, mainly French but also other nationalities, has risen to 230 and the condition of overcrowding is getting very serious as another 50 evadé's are reported to be on the way to Lérida. A Red Cross representative informs the French that they will be moved as soon as either the prison in Barcelona or the camp at Miranda de Ebro have space for them. No news for us. That night the French are having a terrific sing song, shaking the lice out of the ceiling!

15 October. We write a "round robin" to Consul Kriens in Barcelona.

The next day Linthorst Homan expresses the hope to be leaving on the following Monday and begins sharing out his cakes, cigarettes and chocolates among the rest of us. We also fill more covers with maize-husks so now everyone of our party has two mattresses. We have to fill in a form for the American Red Cross so that payment can be made for our "board and lodgings" to this establishment.

At six in the evening all the Poles and Linthorst Homan depart suddenly but not before he distributes ten packets of cigarettes. We also receive another 50 pesetas pocket money.

17 October. It transpires that the "note for the American Red Cross", and possibly also our fingerprints, were to identify the writer of an anti-

semitic letter which had been circulating. The culprit was found, given eight days solitary but not after receiving a beating from two Spanish inmates[16].

Monday 18 October. Mr Fruin learned from the doctor that we will be leaving for Miranda the next day. In the afternoon two more Dutchmen join our unhappy band. They had crossed the Pyrenees at Andorra in company with 15 American aircrew.

At six [we had] a visit from Piet de Jong with a Spaniard from the consulate to help us to complete the forms for our transit visas for Portugal and a registration form for the embassy in Madrid.

On to Miranda

Piet recounts how they finally left Lleida, with high hopes of better accommodation elsewhere:

Tuesday 19 October. At ten o'clock we see our suitcases being deposited in the courtyard. They were immediately issued to us. The food from the restaurant arrives earlier than usual. Thirty Dutch and 30 French are handcuffed, one to one, in the corridor outside the prison office. Beets stays behind and Theo Wachtel is still in solitary waiting for his haircut.

The first group, all French, have already departed when it is our turn to be shackled and led to the coach. I was connected with my left wrist to Alfred Frank's right and, as fate would have it Nico Gazan, who had such an awful time in the mountains, was handcuffed to the "noble" Chevalier Lagasse de Locht, alias Lathouwers. Arriving at Lérida station we are seen off by Linthorst Homan, Piet de Jong, Charls, Faber and Frans. We are each given a bread roll with a fiery Spanish sausage, a banana and a beret to cover our scalp; then we are loaded into a cattle truck and the doors are slid shut, leaving us in the dark.

We have gained our night vision when the train departs at half past two. To begin with we are in good spirits and morale is high now we have left prison and are in the relatively cleaner goods van, in spite of our British-made handcuffs. Air comes through the louvred ventilators set high in the side of the wagon, which also let in a glimmer of light. Although these railway vans are designed for "eight horses or forty humans" there is

---

16 This sentence does not make sense. We suspect Piet meant to write 'not *before* receiving a beating'.

not enough space on the floor for all to sit down at the same time. So we have to take turns to get a rest. We must have been either a precious or dangerous cargo as it needed 20 Guardia Civil, armed with pistols and automatic guns, to guard us. These gentlemen, with typewriters on their head, did not share the comforts of our compartment but had to rough it in an ordinary carriage added to the goods train.

Half past eight and the train arrives at a siding in Zaragoza. Here the doors are opened a little to give us some fresh air which we gulp in, blinded at first by the evening light. We were also allowed to relieve ourselves through the narrow openings, instead of the corner of our conveyance. Awkward to do using the "wrong" hand.

The reception committee this time consisted of a local Dutch businessman, Mr. Timmermans, and a Mr Davids, unofficial representative of the Embassy. Their news was that we will be released from Miranda on 15 November. Our escort returned and was replaced by another one, but our handcuffs were not taken off. They were counted and an equal number went back with the departing guard[17]. Timmermans and Davids return bringing a basket with rolls filled with warm meat (two per man), a lump of cheese, cigarettes and a basket with 12 bottles of wine, the greater part of which was drunk by our escort.

We have difficulty getting any sleep either sitting on the now rather damp floor or standing up as our wrists were sore from the rubbing handcuffs which being of the ratchet type closed a tooth every time they were knocked. Also the atmosphere in the closed compartment became oppressive because of the insufficient ventilation. The rocking of the unsprung vehicle on the uneven track caused a number to become carsick.

The train stops on the morning of 20 October in the goods yard of Logroño station and this time our doors were slid wide open. Our escort was changed again and the new one was of a more humane disposition as our cuffs are taken from us, returned to the departing guards and not replaced this time. They had made the journey from Lérida to Logroño!

Morale picked up those last 25 miles or so to Miranda as the doors were

---

17 This is confusing – what was counted and sent back with the guard? Piet says their handcuffs were not taken off, but perhaps he means that they were replaced, and the original ones returned. This fits with what he says happened when they reached Logroño: their handcuffs were sent back with the departing guard, 'and not replaced this time'. However, he does say that those handcuffs 'had made the journey from Lérida to Logroño!'

now left ajar, but not wide enough to jump train, improving ventilation and allowing some light to enter our lives.

From the platform at Miranda station we looked down into a valley where nestles the "Campo de Concentracion de Miranda de Ebro"[18] to give it its full name, and it made a good impression with its red tiled roofs on whitewashed barracks, all in neat rows.

---

18 This is rather puzzling, as the area formerly occupied by the camp is on the same level as the railway station.

Chapter 12

Miranda de Ebro

Our journey to Miranda de Ebro was much easier than Piet's: we drove back to Zaragoza, returned the hire car and then took a fast train from the impressive modern Zaragoza station direct to Miranda. We checked into a cheap but decent hotel near the station. Piet and his companions were not so lucky. Their high hopes were dashed, and the initial *good impression* proved to be misleading once the Dutchmen were inside.

> *At the administration barrack, outside the barbed wire enclosure we have to register once more. Spain must be by now bursting at the seams with books registering, time and again, over and over, the names of thousands of illegal entrants from all the nations of occupied Europe.*
>
> *Once inside the enclosure, surrounded by double barbed wire fences and patrolled by armed military sentries, the previous opinion from a distance soon changed to that of abject horror. The stench was unbearable and the filth indescribable.*
>
> *This is not the place to do so. At some future date I may be able to write a sanitised version of my memoirs of the time spent there.*

This part of his travels, the most horrific and harrowing, is also the part he talks about least in this account. However, he did write a briefer account of his adventures for his grandchildren, and in that he is more specific about his experiences in Miranda. Perhaps this is the *sanitised version* he intended to write. In it he says:

Miranda station

Miranda de Ebro

Arriving, after a 36 hour train journey, at the camp of Miranda de Ebro we were allocated a hut after the occupants had been chased out. The hut was designed for 60 people, but by the time more arrivals had joined the complement was 132. We soon got ourselves organised by electing a committee with a chief, purser, interpreter, health caretaker etc. With some 5000 inmates, of all nationalities and many races and religions, many sick and injured people, no sanitation or running water, conditions were indescribable.

Soon, however, the Dutch contingent started taking over the sanitation, de-lousing and health of the camp, as our group had a number of medical students of varying seniority amongst it. Through the Red Cross they obtained medicines, disinfectants and vaccines, and conditions improved gradually. Twice a day there was a number check and flag hoisting with the Spanish national anthem which we had to salute. One day we emptied our accommodation completely and with a mixture of exhausted carbide of lime and whitewash we painted the whole of the inside of our barrack [hut], and that put paid to the lice that lived in all the crevices.

Food and clothing and other goods soon arrived to us every Thursday; this was provided again by the Red Cross and paid for by various Dutch companies, among which was Philips, the electrical goods company[19].

Other reports

Others have left accounts of life in the camp, which emphasise the inhumane and degrading treatment experienced there. Miranda de Ebro concentration camp was originally built after the Spanish Civil War to house Republican prisoners. From 1940 it housed foreign internees who had escaped from Nazi-occupied Europe. But it was not their final destination; inmates were often released after a period of time once authority was received for them to travel on to another country.

In the Tourist Office in Miranda we were shown a book (in Spanish) about the concentration camp (*Historia del Campo de Concentración de Miranda de Ebro (1937-1947)*, by José Angel Fernandez Lopez). There is a short section about the Dutch prisoners there, and we have roughly translated a couple of paragraphs:

---

19 This is interesting, in view of Piet's comment that one of his companions was a director of Philips (see Chapter 11).

Miranda de Ebro concentration camp

An important colony of Dutchmen passed through this camp during the war years. Many of them came to Spain aided by compatriots belonging to the Dutch Army operating in the south of France together with the French Resistance.

At the beginning of 1943, 100 Dutchmen were registered in Miranda, forming a tight-knit group. In the summer of 1943 their number dropped considerably, many leaving the camp bound for the Dutch colonies of Curaçao and Suriname. Months later the figure increased again when a group of 30 young Dutchmen (five of them Jewish) were brought to Miranda; they had stayed for six weeks in prison in Lleida in difficult conditions. Their stay in Miranda seemed to them much more bearable than that which they had endured in Lleida, although in this camp they had to endure a harsh winter in conditions undoubtedly the toughest that they had ever experienced.

The group of '*30 young Dutchmen*' must be Piet's group, although they spent less than six weeks in Lleida. The writer says that they found Miranda more tolerable than Lleida, although according to Piet it was even worse.

A letter from Israel

A personal account of life in Miranda was given in a letter from Haifa, Israel, written by Piet's companion Alfred Frank on hearing of Piet's death in 2003.

Dear family Schagen,

The sad news reached me and I want to express my condolences to all of you. You shall be surprised that I also wish to congratulate you, for your life shall continue in the sign of a splendid memory.

I left Holland in October 1941 and I went to Switzerland. I left Switzerland in September 1943 and crossed the Pyrenees together with Piet. When we reached Spain we remained together and when the Spanish Guardia Civil brought us in a bus to the prison in Lerida (Lleida), as there was no room for all of us in the bus, Piet and I volunteered to sit in the open air on the roof of the bus.

We came together from Lleida to Miranda, where I spent the first fortnight in the Red Cross hospital, for in the Lleida prison I got a severe lice infection. When I left the hospital, Piet told me that he reserved one place for me in the barrack, together with another Jewish friend called Leo Hollander, who lives also in Israel. What Piet did in Miranda was wonderful. He got 10 English cigarettes from me, and bought in exchange a stick to walk. He sometimes helped me up and down in the barrack – we were living on the first floor. Once I fell through to the ground floor in the middle of the rice our neighbours prepared, and Piet had to pick me up literally and repair the damage. He also constructed a bottle he broke and connected with tubes he found, and fixed the whole construction outside the barrack in order to enable Leo Hollander to piss during the night without waking us up.

Once we had a peculiar incident in Miranda. On a certain date we were visited by the Allied ambassadors. And to honour them we all stood on parade, we Dutchmen dressed in the biggest dirt we could find in order to show the Dutch ambassador the truth in the camp. Afterwards the Spanish commander announced that the next day there would be a visit from the enemy ambassadors, and the leader of the vast majority of French prisoners informed him that no prisoner was prepared to stand parade for the enemies. The Spanish agreed but informed the camp that the slightest blood on a finger of the ambassadors would entitle the Spanish guards to fire wherever they wanted – so we decided to remain in our barrack the whole day. Piet said this was not enough, so he found remnants of dirty rags outside and constructed a Dutch flag.

Everything went all right, but suddenly there was a knock on the door and a Spanish guard entered with a German officer in uniform. We were ordered to stand in the passage of the barrack in two rows and then the German began his speech. He said that he, as a German, had to honour the enemy when he was victorious and as all of us succeeded to cross the German occupied territory we were the victorious enemy. But, he asked us, where are you now – in a Spanish camp; you do not even know when to get out and how. He therefore had a proposal: all those of us who agreed, would be released now and would spend two weeks in a 5 star hotel in Madrid on the account of the German Embassy. Then everyone would get train tickets and we would return to Holland. Before our journey to Holland everyone would get a written consent of being freed from any labour in Holland or in Germany or in any occupied different territory. Only the Jews, he said, can die in England. And thereupon he wanted to ask everyone personally whether he agreed to accept his proposal.

The first he applied to said "I am Jewish". The second one said "I am also Jewish". Piet was the fifth and he was also Jewish. The German ran out of the barrack and we blockaded the door.

But I remember Piet mainly because of his violent reaction against anti-Semitism amongst the Engelandvaarders. He told me that he was educated by his parents to see no differences in races and he was very angry when he noticed different inclinations.

May God bless his memory. Shalom to all of you, Alfred.

This letter gave us a fascinating glimpse of Piet's life in Miranda, and tells us of an incident we would otherwise know nothing about. It gives some valuable insights into Piet's character. He did not wish to write much about the awful conditions in the camp; and he remained modestly silent about the actions he took to help his fellow prisoners. It is good to know that the squalid conditions in the camp did not manage to break the spirits of the inmates.

Finding the camp

The contrast between the descriptions of the concentration camp and the present day town of Miranda de Ebro could not be greater. The modern town near the railway station has a wide pedestrianised shopping street with outdoor cafés, while the old town on the banks of the Ebro has a restored castle, narrow streets and an impressive convent on the hillside.

Although Miranda is not a major tourist destination, it has enough interesting sites to explore for a few hours. However, the concentration camp is not well marked. At the Tourist Office they did have information and books about the camp, but it is not featured on the tourist trail.

We asked a few people for guidance, but their responses were all vague. Eventually we tracked down the location of the camp, a short walk from the railway station. After some exploration we found a high concrete wall with strands of rusting barbed wire on top. Following this round we came to an old gate, where we could peer through and see that the area inside the wall, though extensive, was heavily overgrown and largely devoid of buildings. Carrying on, we reached a corner where the wall now ran on the steep banks of a small stream. Crossing the stream, we were able to follow the wall on the far bank.

At the next corner we were able to cross the stream on a railway line, and found a monument to the Republican prisoners who were held there after the Spanish Civil War. It was rather battered and clearly not much visited, but was the first real evidence we had that this was actually the site

The wall

of the camp. Walking on we met a Belgian couple who were on a similar
mission – they were researching the place because the man's father was
a Republican prisoner there in 1939. We exchanged notes, and they told
us that there was an information board and a couple of ruined buildings
a bit further on.

This information board also had seen better days. It did tell us that
nearby was the base of a watch tower, the shell of the wash house and
the guard's quarters, all outside the main wall. We found all these, but
they were in poor shape and covered in graffiti. There was no sign of the
barracks and other buildings that used to occupy the space inside the
walls – all was desolate wasteland, except for an oil depot which had been
built at the station end of the complex.

The layout of the camp, as it once was, is described in the following
extract from a scholarly article:

> *The layout of some internment centers was also typically modern: Miranda*
> *de Ebro, one of the central concentration camps, adopted a typical camp*
> *configuration, with rows of parallel blocks surrounded by barbed wire and*

Map of the camp on the battered sign outside

The toilet block

The guard room

sentry boxes. It occupied 42 hectares and was designed for 1,500 prisoners, but the figures soon doubled.[20]

A diagram of the camp layout is on display at the Resistance Museum in Toulouse (see Chapter 6).

While the Nazi extermination camps such as Auschwitz have been maintained as centres of pilgrimage and education, the sizeable complex at Miranda de Ebro is now empty and overgrown, unknown and unvisited except by relatives of those who once were imprisoned there.

---

20 *The Archaeology of Internment in Francoist Spain (1936-1952), by A. Gonzalez-Ruibal, (https://www.academia.edu/3353030/The_Archaeology_ of_Internment_in_Francoist_Spain_1936-1952_)*

Chapter 13

Living Free in Madrid

In his book about the Miranda camp (see Chapter 12), Lopez writes:

In mid-December 1943, 120 Dutch prisoners were released and transferred to Madrid. For six weeks they rested and did nothing, with all their needs covered by the Dutch organization in Madrid. They underwent security checks, were questioned and on 31 January 1944 went by train to Lisbon to sail for Gibraltar and England. This was one of the Dutch convoys of military age to arrive in England before the invasion of Normandy.

Piet describes their departure from Miranda:

My release from internment came on 20 December, exactly two months to the day after the camp had opened its gates to me. I was in comparatively good physical condition, thanks to the provisions made by our Consular and Diplomatic Services, and I shudder to think what would have been my shape had I, like so many others in Spanish captivity, been stateless with nobody caring or taking responsibility for them; bar the International Red Cross.

Whilst interned there I took the opportunity to have my "going away" outfit fumigated, disinfected and laundered. This consisted of my best set of underwear, socks, shirt and tie, pullover, handkerchief and a pair of light trousers. This was sealed in a large biscuit tin with gummed tape.

Dressed in these and wearing Dutch army boots I must have looked quite the dandy compared to some of my fellow liberated prisoners. Some 30 Hollanders went into the little town of Miranda de Ebro.

I went first in search of a barbershop for a shave and a haircut. Since the last one in Lérida, some 2½ months earlier, my scalp had grown a stubble and I hoped that a "short back and sides" would show up the rest to greater advantage. Facial growth disappeared under the capable hands of the barber who must have dealt with a number of internees on previous releases, as his was the first such establishment into town. Looking in the mirror I was pleased with the result.

We had been advised to have new passport photos made, as the ones taken in the camp were not of a suitable quality or appearance to grace our newly issued passports. For lack of a jacket I borrowed a coat and so attired I looked quite presentable on the new photo. Railway tickets had already been issued together with the time of departure of the night express from San Sebastian to Madrid. Long before departure time we were all assembled at the station, lest being left behind. It was first class – we travelled like lords on golden yellow cushion. There was a conspicuous absence of talk in my compartment; most would have been wrapped up in their own thoughts and overcome by the occasion. We must have passed, or even halted at Burgos but I was one who didn't notice it as Morpheus had me in his arms till we arrived in Madrid.

Alfred Frank   Pieter Schagen   Nico Gazan

Louis Van Coevorden   Marcel Wachtel   'Johnnie' Hart

Portraits of 6 Dutch escapers

Before leaving Miranda de Ebro and heading for Madrid, we walked round the area of town close to the site of the camp, in the hope of finding the barber shop where Piet had his trim. Most of the buildings in that area are quite modern, however; only a couple looked as if they dated back to the 1940s, and there was no indication that one of these was once a barber's shop. We left Miranda and caught the train to Madrid.

Arrival in Madrid

At Madrid Estacion del Norte terminus we were met by someone who took us to the Netherlands Consulate in the Claudio Coëllo, there to be issued with a certificate of identity with the new photo and the number of our new passport on it. We were also directed to the hotels where we would be staying. I was allocated to the "Hotel Internacional" in the Calle Arenal (Sand Street) 9, right in the centre of the city.

The certificate of identity had to be taken to the Headquarters of the "Seguridad", situated in the Puerto del Sol, Madrid's main square, just round the corner from the hotel. There I received my Aliens Registration document dated 21 December 1943. With it went the instruction to report there every Thursday for the time I was staying in Madrid. I was free to move within the bounds of the city; but had to obtain prior permission to move outside the capital.

At the Consulate we were given 90 pesetas per week pocket money and a "chit" to the value of 250 pesetas to be spent in the large department store "El Corte Inglès" (The House of England) in the Preciados, one of the posh shopping streets of Madrid. My purchases consisted of a blue double breasted two-piece suit, two shirts, a tie, socks – one pair black silk, which I still have, a pair of black shoes, an overcoat, handkerchiefs, a white towelling bathrobe and lastly a grey trilby hat.

All my old possessions: clothes, army boots, haversack and water bottle, etc., no longer needed, I sold on the second hand market. They had served me well during my trek from Holland, through Belgium, France and across the Pyrenees to prison and camp in Spain. Now in my new outfit I had no further use for them. Anyway I hoped that before long I would be dressed again in uniform. These goods realised unimagined high prices in a poor country that so recently had come out of a devastating civil war. For

Piet and Marcel Wachtel in Madrid

my haversack with army water bottle and the well-worn army boots I was offered an exorbitantly high price.

Our train into Madrid arrived at Chamartin station – Estación del Norte is no longer a functioning railway station but has been converted into a shopping mall. We explored it during the five days we spent in Madrid, tracking down the places Piet mentions in his account.

Piet was taken to the Dutch consulate in Calle Claudio Coëllo, but he does not give a number for the building. We walked along the street, which is close to the Retiro park, but were unable to spot any sign that the consulate was once located there. (Jumping ahead, further research did establish the old address of the Dutch consulate in the 1940s – it was at number 25 Calle Claudio Coëllo.)

In moving from the concentration camp of Miranda de Ebro to the

Estación del Norte

Hotel Internacional in Madrid, Piet went from one extreme of luxury and comfort to the other. We found the hotel in Calle Arenal, and discovered it was an imposing structure covered in ornate baroque carvings and statues. It no longer functions as a hotel but has been converted into upmarket flats. Back in 1943 it must have been an impressive address for a wandering refugee.

The old Dirección General de Seguridad building was pointed out to us in Puerto del Sol, and it is an imposing edifice which once housed Franco's feared security organisation. Nearby, El Corte Inglès still functions as Madrid's premier department store, with an extensive menswear department.

I met Frans again in Madrid. He left Lérida shortly after us by normal train and was now staying in "Hotel Nueva York" in the Avenida José Antonio, named after one of Franco's war heroes – but now as before renamed the "Gran Via". In the same hotel were also Charls and Faber. Together we explored the city with its many attractions, like the Prado with its many old masters, the Retiro park with its animal collection and boating lake. I had my first ride on the top deck of a double decker bus.

We found the location of the now defunct Hotel Nueva York in Gran Via, and also

Hotel Internacional

Seguridad office, Puerto del Sol

Retiro Park

visited the Retiro park, although we were familiar with it from a previous visit. Similarly, we had been to the Prado before, but visited again during free evening admission in order to see the Goyas and other magnificent paintings.

The lost swimming pool

Several times a week we took the tram down to the river Manzanares, where there was an indoor swimming-pool; no mixed bathing and full bathing costume with bathing cap required. Things have changed a little since those days, judging by the "undress" at the bathing beaches these days. Another thing that was taboo then was kissing in public.

This passage gave us the biggest headache we had in tracing the places Piet mentions in Madrid. Unlike many other major cities, the river in Madrid is not an important feature and does not flow through the city, but rather round it to the west and south. However, finding an indoor swimming pool located at the river should not have been a problem – but it was. The main Tourist Office in Plaza Mayor could find no trace of such a pool. Another Tourist Office was slightly more helpful, and told us of a pool situated close to the river which might be the one mentioned.

We found the pool, located in the area of the university, but decided it was too far from the river to be the one described by Piet. It was also tightly locked up and surrounded by a high hedge, so it was hard to tell if it was still functioning. We walked down to the river, which in this section flows to the west of the city, and walked along the bank, looking for any building which might once have been a swimming pool. The river there is shallow and the surrounding area slightly rundown. Needless to say, we found no sign of the pool we were looking for.

Later on we visited the river to the south of the city, which has been 're-formed' and the area smartened up with gardens, lawns, footpaths and bridges. We did see one building which resembled a swimming pool from the outside, but it turned out to be an old slaughterhouse!

We had no luck searching for the pool on the ground, so decided to try a different tack. We went to the Madrid Historical Museum, but the exhibits there dated from the 19th century or earlier. However, the assistants suggested we try the Historical Library, in Conde Duque, outside the city centre. It was the weekend, and the library did not open until Monday, the day we were leaving Madrid. But we could not bear to miss a final opportunity to track down the swimming pool; getting up early and delaying our departure until the afternoon would give us just enough time for a visit to the library.

Accordingly, we travelled on Monday morning to Conde Duque, an old building with a large central courtyard containing various municipal offices, including the Historical Library. We hoped that staff in such a place would speak some English, but were disappointed. After registering and being issued with another set of reader's cards, we met one of the staff to whom we explained our mission as best we could in Spanish. Eventually he suggested that we needed to consult the city almanac of 1944, which was on microfilm in another building. He wrote out the name of the archive we needed to consult.

We followed his directions to a different building in the same complex, and had to explain our errand again, but now with the name of what we needed written down. A woman took us to a microfilm reader, inserted the relevant roll, and left us to it. Reading microfilm is a fairly delicate operation, and we were rather rusty at it, tending to skid off all over the place at the slightest touch on the knobs. There were hundreds of pages of information, listing everything about Madrid in 1944, including every kind of business and organisation. We found the full address of the Dutch consulate, as well as the British Embassy, and then a section headed '*Piscinas*' (swimming pools). There were only two entries for 1944, but one had an address which was the banks of the Manzanares River. Eureka! We noted down the name ('La Isla'), thanked the archive attendant, and hurried back to our flat and the laptop.

We googled 'Madrid swimming pool La Isla' and found an article about 'The Lost Swimming Pools of Madrid', which contained a section about La Isla:

> *Luis Gutiérrez Soto in 1931 built one of the rationalist jewels lost in Madrid. On one of the islands of the river Manzanares he designed a public pool with three pools. The island was shaped like a ship and consisted of a bathing area in the fore and aft; furthermore, the indoor pool was within the central command bridge. There were cafeteria and changing rooms. The water came from the river and was filtered and chlorinated. The success with the locals was immediate.*
>
> *Just five years later, in the summer of 1936, the Civil War began. The front of Madrid soon reached the outskirts of that area and a nationalist shell impacted on the building of the Island. The offices of the pool were rebuilt after the war, but the overflow of the river in 1947 again damaged it, and finally in 1954 it was closed permanently. A dam was opened and the river islet disappeared[21].*

Our persistence had paid off. We had not found Piet's swimming pool, because it no longer existed. But we had documentary evidence – and even a photograph! – proving that it had existed in 1943-4. Once again, we had proved the accuracy of Piet's account.

La Isla swimming pool

---

21   See also: https://vramon1958.wordpress.com/2014/04/11/la-arquitectura-perdida-de-madrid-una-isla-en-el-manzanares/ with more detail but in Spanish.

The British Embassy

Continuing his description of his life in Madrid, Piet says:

> *The Reading Room at the British Embassy was another popular place to visit, as there we could gather all the possible information about the nation, and its language, we hoped to join in the very near future.*

Finding the British Embassy in Madrid should have been straightforward, but tracking down the place that Piet frequented proved to be more of a challenge. We discovered that it had moved out of the city centre to a tower block on the northern outskirts. Taking the metro there, we breezed happily into reception expecting a reasonable welcome as British citizens. No such luck – once we had fought our way through security, we were informed that we could not get into the actual embassy without an appointment. Eventually the receptionist phoned through to someone and transmitted the basic information we wanted – the address of the previous building.

The current British embassy

There was no way of finding anyone to talk to about the history of the embassy during the war, so we had to be content with that.

Returning to the centre, we eventually tracked down the previous embassy building in Calle de Fernando Santo. It was closed up, with a high fence and a big notice saying that the embassy had now moved out to its new location in the suburbs. What we did notice, however, was that the building itself was a fairly modern-looking circular concrete edifice which looked more recent than the 1940s. It seemed clear that the place Piet visited was not this building either, though it might have been on the same site.

More internet research yielded information about the wartime British Embassy. We found a piece by Maurice Vila about his experiences in Spain during the war, and he describes the Madrid embassy:

> *The embassy was a large solid building with a Spanish style interior courtyard big enough for a lawn and a few trees. At the other end was a large garage and hall which had been converted into a dormitory to accommodate the constant arrivals of escapees – not all of them British – from France*[22].

The Hospital

Piet moves on to matters medical:

> *I paid some visits to comrades in hospital. Nico Gazan was there with a diagnosed kidney complaint, which was, no doubt, the cause of his exhaustion on the climb through the mountains. He was receiving "tender loving care" from his nurses Pilar and Celita, as well as from the switchboard operator Adriana. It was sister Pilar who shed rivers of tears when we came to collect him on his discharge. In London he was declared unfit for military service but reunited with his wife who had followed him from Switzerland.*
>
> *A visit to the dentist cost me four teeth as officialdom would not foot the bill for treatment and fillings; extraction was cheaper. Unfortunately I did not have the wherewithal myself to pay for the right treatment.*

Piet does not say which hospital his comrades were in, but a search on the internet suggested that the Reina Sofia building, opposite the Atocha railway station, was the city's general hospital in the 1940s. Now it serves as one of Madrid's major art galleries, and we visited it one evening while free admission was in force. The modern art on display was interesting and impressive, but it was also fascinating to wander the high arched corridors and imagine them filled with hurrying doctors and bustling nurses in days gone past.

---

22 See: http://www.bbc.co.uk/history/ww2peopleswar/stories/31/a7855031.shtml

Corridors of the Reina Sofia

Christmas and New Year

The time Piet spent in Madrid covered Christmas and the New Year.

On Christmas Eve several of the residents of Hotel Internacional went to the beautiful Cathedral of San Francisco to Midnight Mass, Catholic or not, to celebrate the coming of Christmas and the freedom that had come to us. My new shoes hurt my feet, who for so long had been used to the roomy army boots. So after leaving the church when the service was over I took them off and walked back to the hotel in my socks, using as much as possible the tram rails set in the cobbled streets. That night I left my shoes soaking in the washbasin to make them more pliable, and they caused me no more grief after that.

I discovered later that there was also a Protestant church in Madrid.

Piet was never renowned for religious fervour, and his family came from a Protestant area of Holland[23]. However, the service in the impressive

---

23   Notes of his interrogation in London state that he was not baptised; his father was Dutch Reformed, his mother Lutheran.

Cathedral of San Francisco

basilica clearly was a memorable occasion for him. The main cathedral in Madrid is newer and close to the Royal Palace, but we paid a visit to the basilica of San Francisco, and were able to admire its soaring dome and brilliantly decorated interior.

New Year's Eve in the hotel was a memorable occasion, as the photographs then taken show, and is to this day remembered by those who attended. One lady of my acquaintance lost her fiancé for most of the evening.

It sounds like a pretty good party. We have a copy of one of the photos taken, with Piet smiling at one side and a crowd of forty or fifty, mostly men, who look as if they are having a jolly time.

A trip to Toledo

A group of us obtained permission to make an excursion to Toledo, the ancient former capital of Spain, escorted by a Madrid policeman in mufti.

New Year's Eve 1943 (Piet is on the extreme left)

Among the sights was the Cathedral with its treasure chamber, containing the first 24 pounds of gold from the Americas, reputedly brought back by Columbus. The richness displayed in the treasury contrasted with the poverty outside the Cathedral with begging urchins.

El Greco's villa, where there were some of his paintings on display, impressed me, as did the Moorish style of the Synagogue, a former Mosque. The Alcazar was in ruins after its siege during the civil war and was nothing much more than a heap of rubble. Today it is beautifully restored to its former glory. A visit was made to a shop and workplace where the famous Toledo steel blades were still made; we had a demonstration of its efficiency. More attractive was the damascene work which I much admired. Unfortunately lack of funds prevented me from purchasing even a very small item. Too soon came the time for our return to Madrid, but I was lucky enough to manage a second visit to this enchanting walled city; encouraging me to make another visit many years later.

We visited Toledo on our way from Madrid, travelling by train from Atocha station. The cathedral is certainly impressive, and in the treasury is an enormous gold monstrance, which may be the gold that Piet refers to. There were no beggars outside, however. The Alcazar is a huge square building with a tower at each corner, clearly rebuilt relatively recently, but not open to the public.

Toledo   *Santa Maria la Blanca synagogue*

We visited the El Greco villa, though we noted it was not actually his home, but a later reconstruction by someone who tried to replicate what he thought the villa would have been like. It has a number of paintings but not many by the artist himself – others are by his assistants or his son. But the style, with the gaunt ethereal figures, is unmistakeable and makes them stand out from conventional religious art of the time.

There are actually two synagogues open to the public near the El Greco house. One is Santa Maria la Blanca, which is small but full of white Moorish-style columns and quite lovely. The other one, called Transito, is less beautiful by has some nice Islamic-style plasterwork. We also passed dozens of shops selling Toledo steelwork, including racks of swords of all shapes and sizes.

In Toledo we hired a car, ready to follow Piet as he left Madrid on his way into Portugal.

Chapter 14

Portugal and Gibraltar

t last the day came for the refugees to leave their gilded cage in Madrid and move on.

It was late in January 1944 when finally the long awaited transit visas for Portugal arrived and I received my new passport (nr.33562) and was now ready to continue the journey. But before my passport, papers, documents, instructions et al were handed over I had to sign a bond to repay to the State all the monies expended on my behalf by the Netherlands Authorities during my sojourn in Spain. This came to a staggering sum – in Spanish pesetas! A chink of light came when we found out that we would be let off paying this debt if we joined the Dutch armed forces once in Britain. It was H.M. Queen Wilhelmina who had instituted a decree to this effect. The last reporting stamp on the reverse of my Aliens Certificate bore the date of 28 January 1944, the day before our departure from Madrid.

Some 120 Engelandvaarders were assembled early in the morning of 29 January at the Estacion del Sur in the Atocha to entrain for an as yet unknown destination. Unnecessary to say that no one was late for this appointment. We were seen off by the staff, regular and voluntary, of Embassy and Consulate and also many who hoped to follow us soon. Frans was there and so was the lady to see off her fiancé.

Our departure from Madrid also took place from the Atocha station, which has a really beautiful old section with a kind of indoor jungle. The main problem there was finding out how to buy tickets, which proved to be quite a challenge.

Into Portugal

> *The doors of the compartments stayed firmly locked during our journey through Spain until the train reached the first station inside Portugal at Elvas. To continue our journey on Portuguese track we had to change trains as their gauge differed from the much wider Spanish one. Whilst on the platform we were addressed by the leader, Ritmeester (Captain of Horse) Pahud de Mortanges[24], the Olympic Equestrian Champion, who there and then put the whole group officially under Netherlands Military Law. When the train departed the doors stayed unlocked.*

From Toledo we drove south and west, and crossed the border at Elvas, where we stayed the night. Elvas is a beautiful old fortified city, with yellow city walls and a towering old aqueduct. It was the base from which the Duke of Wellington launched his attack on the Spanish city of Badajoz, just over the border, during the Peninsular War.

Our main task was to find the railway station; it is a little way out of town and is no longer used for passenger trains, though freight trains still rumble through. We went onto the long platform and found the station building was covered with a number of beautiful blue tile pictures of the city. Two young women, artists from Lisbon, were working on the tiles to restore the pictures to their former glory. Chatting to them, we found there were plans to re-open the station and start passenger trains again – hence the restoration of the tiles. We hope these plans will come to fruition soon.

Elvas station

Restoring the murals

---

24   See https://en.wikipedia.org/wiki/Charles_Pahud_de_Mortanges for more information about this individual.

At the beginning of the previous chapter, we quoted from Lopez:

120 Dutch prisoners were released [from Miranda de Ebro] and transferred to Madrid ... on 31 January 1944 [they] went by train to Lisbon to sail for Gibraltar and England.

Frans later went to the UK via Lisbon, and this was what Piet and his companions expected to do, as the train took them west through Portugal. But they were in for a surprise.

Initially the train went in the direction of Lisbon and some of us had visions of flying from there to Britain but just before reaching the capital the train went south till we reached the Atlantic at the south coast, now better known as the Algarve. There we turned east along the coast back in the direction of Spain where we stopped at the little fishing village of Vila Real de Santo Antonio on the right bank of the Guadiana river, which forms the border between Portugal and Spain.

Vila Real de Santo Antonio

As we had never visited the Algarve, we decided to take a few days' break from our quest to do so, ending up at Vila Real de Santo Antonio (often abbreviated to VRSA) after exploring the rest of the coastline. Piet's description of it as 'a little fishing village' did not prepare us for the modern reality of the place, a busy, bustling and traffic-clogged town where we struggled to park and find our hotel. There is a pedestrianised town centre around a market square, where black and white cobbles form lines which radiate out from the centre. There is also a riverside walk, with views across to Spain.

We found the attractive art deco station on the outskirts of town, where the 120 Dutchmen would have arrived. We checked online and found it was built in 1936, so they would have seen the same building.

We were billeted, some of us in the village hall, where I slept on a mattress on the dance floor. After depositing our luggage we explored the village. This did not take much time as there was nothing much to see or do except

VSRA station

to have another haircut. The only activity was at the sardine canning factory, situated on the quayside and where was moored a ship being loaded with crates of the tinned sardines. She was a beautiful ship with the lines of a schooner with two raked masts and flying the Merchant Navy red flag from the stern. Her name was "Sayonara" ("Farewell" in Japanese). Moving about her and in the village I noticed some men in flared trousers and white shirts and thought them to be fishermen in local costume.

We were left with two more places to find: the 'village hall' where Piet slept, and the canning factory and dock where the ship was moored. In the town we had already noticed a very smart market hall, now a cultural centre, with a craft market inside but clearly used for other functions as well. A nearby poster said that the place was originally a barracks, later a market place. It was definitely there in 1944, although it seemed rather too smart to be called the 'village hall'. But we saw no alternatives, and certainly the location fitted with Piet's narrative, as it is central and from there it is easy to explore the town and waterfront.

Finding the canning factory and dock was more of an issue. We went to the library, and a helpful woman there showed us old photos of the town's factories, and said they were along the river to the south of the town, towards the sea. But now the sardine canning industry was

Old canning factory

defunct, and the factories were all abandoned. We walked there anyway and saw many derelict buildings which used to be canneries in the last century. However, they were a long way from the town centre, and the water seemed too shallow for a ship to be moored nearby. And why does Piet talk as if there was only one canning factory, when in fact there were several?

We attempted to talk to some fishermen, in order to solve this puzzle. They called over a friend, whose English was good – fortunate as we do not speak any Portuguese! He told us he was a communist, and talked about the canning industry and its decline; he said there was just one old factory close to the town centre, and told us how to find it. We walked back along the quayside, and just before the centre we found a set of ruined buildings not far back from the river. What is more, there was a dilapidated jetty in the river just opposite the derelict factory, and we realised this was very likely the spot where 'Sayonara' tied up to load the cases of sardines. This was yet another example of searching for and finding a place matching Piet's account – thanks to our communist fisher friend.

We boarded her very early the next morning, 30th January. 120 Dutch and 28 Polish escapers were packed into her like the sardines she was carrying. We were constantly in the way of the crew who were not backward to

The jetty

teach us the finer expressions and points of the English language which our masters had failed to teach us at school. Because of lack of space my station was under the table in the dining room together with I do not know how many others.

At sea, and once we were at three miles outside Portuguese territorial waters, there came a change on board. First the "Red Duster" came down and was replaced by the "White Ensign" of the Royal Navy. The bellbottomed sailors smartened up and wore navy hats with a ribbon and a bow. The officers re-appeared with gold braid on the sleeves of their jackets. The covers came off guns and automatic weapons and we found ourselves on board of ABV (Auxiliary Boarding Vessel) HMS "Sayonara", whose normal duty was to patrol the Atlantic side of the Straits of Gibraltar to intercept neutral ships and search them for contraband destined for the enemy. It took 21 hours and 11 minutes, according to the log, to reach "Gib". Many years later I did some research into the history of the ship resulting in some surprises.

It is not clear what the surprises were, as Piet does not explain this. Looking up the ship on the internet[25] showed that it was launched in 1911, requisitioned by the Royal Navy in 1939 and sold in 1946.

---

25   See: http://uboat.net/allies/warships/ship/13690.html

The Sayonara

Short of chartering our own vessel, we failed to find any way of sailing from VRSA to Gibraltar, so were forced to drive round via Spain. We crossed the frontier again and drove via Huelva and Seville to reach La Linea, at the border with Gibraltar. There we handed back the car and walked across with our luggage, to reach the British territory of 'The Rock', the last staging post in Piet's journey to England.

Gibraltar

We arrived at Gibraltar in the dark and had to stay outside in the bay as the harbour was closed till daylight. There were loud underwater explosions during that time to deter enemy frogmen from planting limpet mines on the hulls of the Allied ships at anchor.

Disembarkation followed at daybreak and the Dutch contingent was marched off a little way up the hill to Saint Mary's School, which was to be our home for the duration of our stay on the Rock. The Polish escapers were housed in the casemates of "Moorish Castle", a short distance away.

Our Officer in Charge was the "Ritmeester". Soon we were marched to the quartermaster's store to be issued with a kitbag, British Army battledress and other equipment but no boots, of which there was a shortage. How I regretted having disposed of my Dutch army [boots] in Madrid as civilian shoes do not go very well with army gaiters.

The Rock was swarming with service personnel of all three services,

Approach to the rock

British as well as foreign, male and female. The civilian population had been evacuated to Britain for the duration and the only civilians allowed were the Spanish workers who came in the morning and had to leave again at dusk.

Our first challenge in Gibraltar was to find the wartime location of St Mary's School. We found the current school easily enough, but it was not as described by Piet *'a little way up the hill'*. We went to the tourist information office and explained our quest to a young woman. *'Hang on'*, she said, *'I'll call my mother – she was at school there'*. After speaking to her mother, she returned to us and described the school's previous location – a little way up the hill, as Piet said. We passed the place later and found it had been converted into flats.

The casemates where the Poles were billeted were probably in Casemates

St Mary's School

Square, at the entrance to the main street. These are connected by old walls to the actual Moorish Castle higher up.

We were kept busy, and entertained, with lectures on various military subjects, hygiene and drill. Those of us who had held a military rank in the past were allowed to wear the equivalent badges of rank. And very proudly we wore the Netherlands flashes on our sleeves. The drill was so that the untrained among us could be moved about in a more or less military manner. The new recruits were quicker in the uptake than those who had longer or shorter training in a different drill, sometimes to great hilarity and frustration of our instructors.

Water was in short supply and we had to get used to having two taps; one for drinking water and the other supplying salt seawater. We also experienced douching and washing with saltwater and a special kind of soap that was supposed to lather but didn't.

There were periods of free time in the day and evening and we could visit the camp cinema as well as the Navy one. In the theatre the "Garrison Players" performed a pantomime called "Alf's Button on the Rock", a bawdy version of "Ali Baba" with an all male cast, to the great approval of the audience.

We were told where the theatre used to be during the war, but it is now an open square – the building has been demolished. We could not identify the camp and navy cinemas – perhaps these were temporary locations.

Although still February I had a swim in the sea at Catalan Bay in amongst the barbed wire sea defences.

We walked round to the east side of the peninsula to reach Catalan Bay, a pleasant small sandy beach with the cloud-capped Rock towering over it. We were not tempted to swim in the sea, but had a paddle in Piet's memory.

From the windows of our billet, Saint Mary's School, we had a beautiful view of the Bay, Algeciras and La Linea in Spain and the coast of Africa. The Strait was the highway for enormous convoys of ships supplying the Allied forces in the Mediterranean area. There was a constant coming and

Catalan Bay

going, and sometimes it looked as if the same ships went just back and forward for our amusement. We gave up counting them.

Seeing the sights

We had conducted tours, just like the tourists we were, of the Rock and its innards. It was honeycombed with underground passages, gun emplacements, a fully equipped hospital and water reservoir as big as a lake. This was replenished from a catchment area on the west or Mediterranean slope of the Rock.

On the top, where there now is a restaurant at the terminus of the cablecar, was a gun emplacement displaying its name "Virgin's Paradise", no doubt because of the state of undress of the gunners. The number of monkeys, which had decreased, had been augmented, on Winston Churchill's orders, with new blood to keep the legend going.

Tunnels through the rock

There was no black-out on the Rock so as not to stand out from nearby
Spain which sparkled with lights. Once a week, I believe on a Friday, all
the guns were tested and fired causing a terrible din.

Like Piet, we saw the tourist sights. We had a guided tour of the tunnels
used in World War II, with life-size models of the sleeping quarters and

WW2 hospital

Top of the rock – previously Virgin's Paradise

a hospital inside. Further up the rock are the Siege Tunnels, built in the 18th century during the siege by the French and Spanish. We also visited St Michael's Cave, a large natural cavern used for concerts and other performances.

Gibraltar 'ape'

We took the cablecar to the top of the Rock; near the café we found the remains of a gun emplacement, which might even have been the one mentioned by Piet. On the way back down we saw large numbers of the Gibraltar 'apes', which are actually macaque monkeys.

Our departure from Gibraltar came when one day along the South Mole moored a troopship, the "Orduña Castle", a converted freighter of the Castle Line, which had place on board to take us to Britain. With some hilarity we learned how to sling a hammock and to get into it.

We were not allowed to walk out on the South Mole.

The next day, 10 March, the troopship joined another vast convoy, among which we noticed the "Warspite" and also the Dutch liner "Johan van Oldenbarneveldt". We sailed endlessly west, zig-zagging into the Atlantic and then northwards to go round the north of Ireland and enter the Irish Sea and so to Liverpool Docks.

We also left Gibraltar for Britain, but by air rather than sea. On the day, the clouds were too low to allow any planes to land, so we were bussed to Malaga and flew home from there.

Piet had reached the end of his travels through Europe, but he still had some obstacles to overcome before he reached his goal, of joining the forces which were fighting against Hitler.

Chapter 15

Final Destination – London

fter his adventures, Piet finally arrived in war-torn Britain. The troopship docked in Liverpool, then:

After disembarkation we were driven in waiting double decker buses to Lime Street station to board the train to London. Tea chests with sandwiches and bottles of lemonade were brought aboard the train, which we shared with our soldier escort, who confessed that although they carried rifles they had no ammunition with them. Not that it mattered as none of us was likely to run away now we were so close to our goal, London.

Interviews with the security services

That evening we arrive in a "pea-souper", so thick that the conductresses had to walk in front with torches lighting up the kerbs to show the way to the drivers. Eventually we reached "Battersea Grammar School" at Tooting Bec Common. This was the "waiting room" for the "Royal Victoria Patriotic School for Girls" to give it its full title, where in due course our turn would come to be interrogated by members of the Army Intelligence Corps.

To complete our exploration of Piet's odyssey, we took the train to London on 31 October 2015, with a list of the places he mentions when writing about his time there; we explored the metropolis in order to see them for ourselves.

We found the gates with 'Battersea Grammar School' still inscribed upon them, but clearly the building was in new hands. A large sign proclaimed '*Streatham and Clapham High School*', apparently an independent girls' school, and clearly undergoing some major refurbishment. From there we made our way to Wandsworth to find the Royal Victoria Patriotic School for Girls. It was the evening of Halloween as we approached the pile – a slightly eerie experience given its gothic appearance. Wikipedia summarises its history:

> *The Royal Victoria Patriotic Building is a large Victorian building in a "gothic" style combining Scottish Baronial and French Châteauesque. It is located off Trinity Road in Wandsworth, London. It was built in 1859 as the Royal Victoria Patriotic School, by popular subscription as an asylum for girls orphaned during the Crimean War. It is a Grade II* Listed Building designed by the architect Major Rohde Hawkins.*[26]

There was little sign of the building's current function, but we gathered by looking around that it is now mainly upmarket apartments, with at least one bar inside which was advertising Happy Hour, and appropriately was hosting a Halloween party.

Piet describes his interrogation briefly:

Royal Victoria Patriotic School

---

26   See https://en.wikipedia.org/wiki/Royal_Victoria_Patriotic_Building

First we had to state in which language(s) we were proficient enough to be examined. I gave English and Dutch, being confident enough that I could manage in English. It would shorten the process as there were likely to be more English than Dutch speaking interrogators. As it was I was "out" in a few days after having my soap cut in half and my toothpaste tube squeezed empty[27]. But my passport was stamped:

> *"PERMITTED TO LAND*
> *PROVIDED THE HOLDER*
> *JOINS THE DUTCH FORCES"*

After my release from the "Patriotic School", as it became known, I was held in "Florys", a villa on the edge of Wimbledon Common, and being escorted daily to Eaton Square, there to be further interrogated by the Netherlands Security Service about Dutch and local matters, conditions and people.

Unfortunately we were unable to track down 'Florys' or the place in Eaton Square where Piet was questioned by the Dutch authorities. However, we did manage to get copies of transcripts of these interviews. One we found in Amsterdam at the NIOD, and our friend Renée translated it for us. To get access to the other, Renée managed to penetrate the archives of the Dutch security services and find a transcript. As she was not allowed to copy this, she made copious notes and sent us a translation. Details from these transcripts can be found in Appendix A.

Joining the forces

After that hurdle I was billeted in "Zetland House" in South Kensington and had to report to the Netherlands Forces Recruiting Office in Mayfair.

We found our way to Zetland House, which still stands, but we could not find the exact location of the Recruiting Office in Mayfair.

---

27 We do not understand the significance of this, but guess that the authorities were searching every conceivable hiding place for illegal objects. Remember Lathouwers had a rolled-up Dutch passport in his toothpaste tube (see Chapter 9).

H.M. Queen Wilhelmina, renowned to be the only man in the Dutch Government in exile[28], had made the rule that those who had come from occupied Europe to join the Allied Forces had the free choice of service, provided that they were fit and suitable and were accepted for training by that service. Otherwise for those not having sufficient English to be trained there was the "Prinses Irene Brigade", a Dutch Army unit, named after the Queen's second granddaughter born in Canada. Also she received, as soon as practicable, everyone who had arrived, for a "chat" over tea at her home.

Presumably Piet had tea and chat with the Queen, but he does not describe the event.

From a young age I have had this yen to become a flyer, or at least to have something to do with airplanes, and now I had my chance.

At the Recruiting Office I was asked by the officer about my military service, and I declared 4½ years of service with the 21st Infantry Regiment until made a prisoner of war in May 1940, from which I had walked away. I was immediately classed as a regular or professional NCO, in spite of my maintaining that I was a conscript whose service had been extended time and time again because of conditions in Europe in those years[29]. This was not accepted without proof and I was told to return in four days' time to be inducted in the "Brigade Prinses Irene" in Wolverhampton.

I left feeling angry and betrayed and was at a loss where to turn for advice.

Obviously Piet had excellent English. We assume that professional NCOs were needed in the Princess Irene Brigade. He was bitterly disappointed, as he wished to join the RAF. But help was at hand.

In London, at the time, was "Netherlands House" in Charles Street, Mayfair, a Dutch club where Dutch servicemen were welcome, and also "Oranjehaven" in Bayswater Road, a house provided by our Queen as

---

28 We think Piet is being ironic – the Queen was the only tough member of the government, the others were wimps!

29 This is not consistent with the record of his interview with the security services (see Appendix A). There he said that he returned to the army as a volunteer ('capitulant') in January 1938.

a haven for those Engelandvaarders who had no relatives or friends in Britain. There they could meet old comrades, have some light refreshments or enjoy a drink. It is there that I went that afternoon to see who I might find to share my misery with. It was announced by the father of the house that Prins Bernhard would shortly making a visit and wanted to meet those he had not met before, and would they collect in the lounge to await him. It was then that I came in conversation with him and mentioned my earlier experience at the Recruiting Office. He took a note and told me to come the next morning at nine to his office in Arlington House, Arlington Street, behind the Ritz Hotel, and it would be sorted out.

There was no indication in Charles Street of where 'Netherlands House' used to be, but in Bayswater Road it was easy to find 'Oranjehaven', as there is a large plaque on the building which tells all. Arlington House is similarly easy to find, but it is now a complex of smart flats and does not welcome the curious.

Oranjehaven

Oranjehaven sign

As indeed it was, after I was received by his secretary Lieutenant van Brero, a fellow Engelandvaarder, who already knew about my case. He went into an anteroom to make a phone call and returning told me that there would be an RAF Aircrew Selection Board at the former GEC offices in High Holborn.

Attending I was tested for aptitude and English, interviewed and accepted for training as navigator/bomb-aimer and sworn in. It was then discovered that, as an alien, I should not have been asked to swear an allegiance to King George VI as I had already an allegiance to my own Queen. Contact was made with the Netherlands Embassy to enquire as to what my position was. I could have lost my nationality by swearing allegiance to a foreign potentate. Luckily it was considered that I had sworn my allegiance with the permission of the Crown and would not lose my nationality.

Ironically, in 1957 Piet did forsake his Dutch nationality and became a British citizen.

I reported to No.1 Air Crew Reception Centre, Allied Squadron, St Johns Wood, Regents Park, where I was inducted, kitted and started my training with a squad of Dutch cadets, including the lost fiancé.

When we researched the location of the aircrew reception centre in St John's Wood, we discovered it was none other than Lord's cricket ground! Clearly Piet had no knowledge of, or interest in, cricket, but it is nevertheless surprising that he does not mention this famous location. We went to take some photos of the outside, but the public were not allowed inside unless on a tour. The gateman confirmed, however, that Lord's was an RAF reception centre during the war.

RAF recruits (Piet on the left)

The end of the story

In London I met up with Frans again, who after my departure from Madrid had travelled to Lisbon to be flown from there to Bristol arriving some weeks before our ship docked at Liverpool.

Like all escapers he had been received by Queen Wilhelmina, Patroness of the Engelandvaarders, and decorated by her with the (Netherlands) Cross of Merit, the ribbon of which he wore on his sailor's uniform.

Within a short time of "passing out" from the Patriotic School, he was at Dover, where after a very short training he served as a gun-loader on the MGBs (Motor Gun Boats) and was within a fortnight in action off the French coast against the much bigger German E-Boats.

Frans with Queen Wilhemina

So the journey that began at Zaandam station ended with both of them reaching England and fighting against the Nazis, though in different branches of the armed forces.

> *My arrival in London was seven and a half months almost to the day since Frans and I left our hometown of Zaandam in North Holland[30].*
>
> *Engelandvaarders (escapers) are to this day honoured by the present reborn Netherlands Armed Services, who in turn, organise a reunion for those who served the country in wartime. There they meet old comrades from prison days and the services. Prins Bernhard, present patron of the Brotherhood of Escapers, is present on these occasions, if not otherwise prevented.*

Here ends Piet's account of his odyssey through occupied Europe. He did not write any more about his war service and what happened after. Our only source for the rest of his story is family history.

---

30 Piet miscalculated – it was closer to nine months.

Postscript

From a copy of Piet's Dutch military records, we know that he was seconded to the RAF on 25th May 1944. In June 1944 he was involved in a flying bomb explosion in London, which ruptured both eardrums (and left him partially deaf for the rest of his life). He carried on training with the RAF, including a period at Jurby airbase on the Isle of Man. There he met a young Scotswoman from Glasgow, Catherine Craib McMillan (Rena), who was in the WAAF (Women's Auxiliary Air Force) working as a pay clerk.

We have no record of Piet's service in the RAF during the remainder of the war, though we must assume that he flew in bombers as a navigator/bomb-aimer. On 16th November 1945 he married Rena in Jordanhill, Glasgow. It was a double wedding, as Rena's youngest sister Elsie married her husband, Jack Cringle, in the same ceremony.

According to the military records, Piet's secondment to the RAF ended in January 1946 and he was assigned to the Air Force Directorate in London and seconded to the Naval Aviation Service. In May 1946 he was transferred to the Air Force Directorate in the Netherlands. He and Rena moved that year to his home country, and Rena had to adapt quickly to living in a strange land and learning a new language.

On 19th May 1947 their son Ian Pieter Schagen was born in Zaandam. There was an issue about naming him, as traditionally the eldest son in the Schagen family was named Pieter Jacobus, but Rena refused to countenance this. The compromise names of Ian (Scottish) and Pieter (Dutch) were agreed. Although Ian was born in the family town of Zaandam, at this time Piet and Rena were living in Amsterdam, in Sarphatistraat, on the top floor of a four-storey tenement.

In October 1947 Piet went on extended leave from the Dutch military (until his honourable discharge in 1956), and it is probably at this time that he took up a job as an instrument engineer with the Dutch airline KLM, based at Schiphol Airport. Their daughter Margaret Sheila Schagen (Maggi) was born, also in Zaandam, on 10th April 1951.

At some point in 1952 Piet lost his job with KLM, for unknown reasons, and the family left the Netherlands and moved across to Glasgow. They stayed initially with Rena's parents in Jordanhill, and then found a tiny cottage nearby where they lived for about three years. After a while, Piet got a job with British European Airways (BEA – later British Airways), again as an instrument engineer, based at Renfrew airport.

In 1955 BEA moved all its engineering operations to Heathrow airport, near London, and the family moved again, to Bedfont, Middlesex. In August 1957 Piet and the children were naturalised as British citizens. Later they moved to Sunbury-on-Thames, and then to Feltham, but stayed on the western outskirts of London. Piet retired from British Airways in October 1979, and he and Rena lived for a while in Loughborough, Leicestershire, close to Ian and his family. Later they moved to Hook, Hampshire, and lived in sheltered accommodation close to their daughter Maggi.

Rena died of lung cancer in December 1996, and in 1997 Piet wrote his account of his travels through occupied Europe. He began to revisit his roots, travelling back to Holland for meetings of the Engelandvaarders Association, and making contact with some of his former companions. He formed a relationship with the widow of one of these, and they used to travel backwards and forwards to visit each other, though they never married.

Piet died in January 2003, of malignant melanoma.

Key dates

The following timeline is based on Piet's military records, with other key dates inserted.

Date	Event
10/8/1916	Born in Hoorn, Netherlands
4/11/1935	Conscripted into 21st Infantry Regiment
15/2/1936	Entered training as non-commissioned officer (corporal)
13/6/1936	(acting?) sergeant
2/8/1936	Confirmed as sergeant and went on extended leave
24/1/1938	Returned from extended leave / re-entered army as capitulant
5/3/1938	Signed on for six years of military service
15/5/1940	Became PoW after German invasion of the Netherlands
15/7/1940	Demobilised with Dutch Army – extended leave
22/7/1940	Became auxiliary customs officer on Belgian border – Nispen/Ossendrecht
?/5/1942	Left customs post and returned to Zaandam
22/6/1943	Left Zaandam
2/10/1943	Interned in Lleida, then in Miranda de Ebro, Spain
16/3/1944	Arrived in England. Joined Dutch troops in England, based London
25/5/1944	Seconded to RAF. Signed on till 10/8/1956
?/6/1944	Involved in flying bomb explosion – both eardrums ruptured.
16/11/1945	Married Catherine Craib McMillan in Glasgow
4/12/1945	Listed as Reserve Sergeant Observer Bombadier
27/1/1946	Secondment to RAF terminated
28/1/1946	Assigned to the Air Force Directorate London and seconded to Naval Aviation Service
1/5/1946	Relieved of secondment to Naval Aviation Service and transferred to the Air Force Directorate in the Netherlands

19/5/1947	Son Ian Pieter Schagen born in Zaandam
1/9/1947	Business leave for 30 days
25/10/1947	Extended leave
10/4/1951	Daughter Margaret Sheila Schagen born in Zaandam
10/8/1956	Honourably discharged from Dutch Forces
?/10/1979	Retired from British Airways
18/1/2003	Died in Odiham Hospital, Hampshire

Appendix A

Transcripts of interviews with the Dutch authorities

When Piet arrived in London he was interviewed by the British security service, and then by the Dutch authorities. The first Dutch interview dealt with conditions in the occupied countries; later, Piet was interrogated (apparently on two separate occasions) about his family, past history and activities before leaving the Netherlands.

First Dutch interview

We obtained from NIOD (see Chapter 1) notes of the first interview, in Dutch, and our friend Renée translated them for us.

> *Secret*
> *Interrogation April 24th 1944*
> *SCHAGEN,Pieter Jacobus.*
>   *Born at Hoorn: August 10, 1916.*
>   *Residence in the Netherlands: Zaandam*
>   *Left the Netherlands June 22 1943*
>   *Arrival in England March 16 1944*
>   *Occupation Commies customs duties*

Smuggling to Belgium

Speaker worked until the end of 1942 at Customs at the Belgian border, special task: to prevent smuggling. Especially in the first year of the occupation, there was going on an enormous amount of smuggling; in the first place because of the immediate very bad food position in Belgium, and in the second place as a result of the very good food position at that moment in the Netherlands. The Belgian prices were then very high, the Dutch prices relatively low.

The articles being smuggled were: potatoes, grain, butter, cheese, milk powder, sugar, gingerbread cake; in short: all foods. This was the situation up to 1942.

Speaker thought that currently the smuggling is less because, first the food position in Belgium is much better now and in the Netherlands worse than up to 1942, and second the black market in Belgium was much cheaper than the one in the Netherlands.

The north of France

Here the food position is very good and speaker knows there is much smuggling from there to Belgium.

The grain plant of the firm Zwaardemakers at Zaandam is working day and night with three crews. Speaker thinks the grain is mainly destined for the Dutch consumers, although a small part will go to the Wehrmacht. The firm delivers directly to most groceries like Albert Heijn, Haka, Simon de Wit, de Gruyter and others. This goes on allocation coupons.

Fat ration

Speaker estimates that the percentage of margarine (fat of animals) in the share of "fats" is about equal to the percentage of butter people get for one whole year.

The butter that people get on a share coupon has a bad quality and is bad for baking; black crusts remain. The clandestine butter of the farmers is much better and there is less loss. Also the coupon butter goes rancid much sooner.

Coal

> *Is in short supply. Many plants get tree root allocations.*

Piet did not really reveal any secrets of military value, but clearly helped Intelligence to build up a picture of economic life in the occupied countries. The concept of gingerbread smuggling is slightly bizarre, but delightful.

Second Dutch interview

Two days later, Piet was subject to a more probing interrogation into his antecedents and activities – presumably to ensure that he was not a spy or Nazi collaborator. In 2017 Renée managed to gain access to a record of this interview in the archives of the Dutch security services. She was not allowed to copy or photograph it, but made copious notes which she translated for us. These give interesting insights into Piet's family history and his earlier career.

Piet is quoted as giving the following account of his career since leaving school:

> *In 1931 I left the HBS[31] in Zaandam and came into the business of my father, who had an agency of real estate and insurance at that time, and in the meanwhile I was attending the trade school in the evening hours. At the end of 1933 or the beginning of 1934 my father went bankrupt and I found myself a job in 1934 as a shop assistant at Simon de Wit [grocery store] at Koog aan de Zaan.*
>
> > *I was there until November 2nd 1934, and on November 4th 1935[32] I began a framework [basic?] training at the military services of 21 R.I. (infantry regiment) at Amersfoort. On August 1936 I went as a sergeant on extended leave. For a month I was unemployed and then I found myself a job as shop assistant at Albert Heyn at Koog aan de Zaan [also a grocery store]. At the end of 1937 I was fired because I had a big mouth because I earned 5 guilders for one week.*

---

31 Hogere Burger School = higher civilian school.
32 The one year gap seems strange, so perhaps the first date should be 1935.

Presumably he complained about his low wages and got the sack. Piet was never renowned for keeping quiet in the face of perceived injustice. He continues:

> *Meanwhile I received a request of the military services to go back to 21 R.I. as a sergeant-capitulant[33], but my parents were against it. I used the opportunity of my dismissal to go into the military services. On January 24th 1938 I came as capitulant at 21 R.I. at Amersfoort and thereafter I stayed in the military services.*
>
> *During the mobilisation and war I was in the neighbourhood of Woudenberg. My commander there was J. de Vries, brother of the shot-down colonel A. de Vries. On July 18th 1940 I was de-mobilised and was at home for three days.*
>
> *On July 22nd 1940 I became a Commies [customs officer], Import Duties and Excise Duties, located at Nispen. In May 1941 I was transferred to Ossendrecht in the neighbourhood of Bergen op Zoom. I was there until May 1942 and asked for dismissal because we had to work more and more together with the 'Moffen' [a rude name for Germans]. I went home and had all kinds of jobs.*
>
> *On June 22nd 1943 I left the Netherlands together with F. van den Brink, and we travelled together until Lerida where we arrived on October 5th 1943. On October 19th 1943 I was transported to Miranda de Ebro, and I was freed and entered Madrid on December 20th 1943. I left with the big convoy for the UK and I arrived there on March 16th 1944.*

There is a note on the transcript: "A brave Zaankanter [native of the Zaan region]. Politic[ally] reliable."

Apparently at a later date, Piet was interrogated further and gave more details of his actions as a customs officer in Nispen and Ossendrecht.

> *Because of my profession I was armed with a pistol. As we didn't have to hand over the used shells when we used our weapon it was very easy to withhold ammunition, and I did this regularly. I gave this ammunition regularly to two old acquaintances: Jacob Molenaar and Marcus Plooyer.*
>
> *Molenaar was in contact with Ahrends, who was in contact with*

---

33 A conscript who re-entered the army as a volunteer was known as a 'capitulant'. They retained their previous rank, but were initially paid at the same rate as an ordinary soldier.

some non-commissioned officers whose names I don't know. According to Ahrends these officers had weapons but too little ammunition, and he gave the ammunition I had given to Molenaar to these officers. The goal of Ahrends was, in case of an invasion at Zaandam, to keep order together with these officers. About this organisation I do not know anything. I also don't know if Ahrends was the chief of this organisation and if this organisation was a subdivision of the O.D.[34]

Piet also describes what happened to his parents:

My father and mother were arrested by the Germans in August 1942, because of protection of Jews and an anti-German attitude. They were transported to the prison at the Amstelveensweg at Amsterdam. They had been there almost six weeks whereupon they were released.

Piet's parents were fortunate. He describes what happened to a couple of men who shared a cell with his father.

Mr Abraham, an attorney from The Hague – shot because of espionage.
   Mr Veenstra, a dentist from Amsterdam, arrested by the Germans because he gave someone an identity card – transported to Germany.

Sharing his mother's cell was M A Tiggelaar, from Hilversum, who was arrested *'because of listening to forbidden radio stations'*. As well as adding more detail to Piet's story, these transcripts gave an insight into life in the Netherlands under the German occupation.

---

34   Orde Dienst – an important illegal organisation during WW2 in the Netherlands
     See: https://nl.wikipedia.org/wiki/Ordedienst